Go Bears
Frosty

Frosty
IS NO SNOWMAN

KERRY EGGERS

DEMENTI MILESTONE PUBLISHING

Copyright © 2024

All rights reserved. No part of this book may be reproduced or transmitted in any form or by any means, electronically or mechanical, including photocopying, recording, or by any information storage and retrieval system, without the written permission of the Publisher.

Author
Kerry Eggers

Publisher
Wayne Dementi
Dementi Milestone Publishing, Inc.
Manakin-Sabot, VA 23103
www.dementimilestonepublishing.com

Graphic Design
Jayne Hushen

ISBN 979-8-9890973-2-6

Printed in the USA

All profits and donations from the sale of this book will go to the
Oregon State University Foundation for the
COMER FAMILY SCHOLARSHIP
in the support of pharmacy students who are in or have been in the military.

Table of Contents

Dedications: Frosty / Kerry iv
Introduction: In the Blink of An Eye v
Chapter One: The Ghosts of Comertown 1
Chapter Two: Bringing up Frosty 9
Chapter Three: Along Comes Vicki 23
Chapter Four: Goodbye Cruel World, Hello Army 39
Chapter Five: Changing the Drugs Paradigm 53
Chapter Six: Death with Dignity 65
Chapter Seven: Championing Vital Choice 77
Chapter Eight: Bridging the Gulf 89
Chapter Nine: Helter-Skelter in Health Care 105
Chapter Ten: Coram as End-of-Life Forum 117
Chapter Eleven: Cultivating Coram 139
Chapter Twelve: Cook's Recipe for Success 155
Chapter Thirteen: 'Never in Our Wildest Dreams' 165
Chapter Fourteen: Brian's Song an Inspirational One .. 175
Chapter Fifteen: Treating Employees and Customers Right ... 183
Chapter Sixteen: Exploring the Better Half 193
Chapter Seventeen: Frosty: 'A Single Name, Like Madonna' ... 199
About the Author 213
Acknowledgments 214
Index 216

Dedication

To the Comers, Frosty and Vicki, for having faith that I could handle writing a book on a subject way out of my comfort zone.

To my wife Stephanie, for your patience, countenance and love.

KE

To Kerry Eggers, for taking on this Comer family history project.

To my wife of 55 years, Vicki, who has been the rock of our family.

To my two amazing daughters, Wendy and Molly, who then treated us to five amazing grandsons and, so far, one great grandson.

To Brian Cook, who joined our family in his high school years and has added amazing joy to complete us. .

WFC

Introduction

My introduction to the Comer family history came while attending the 101st birthday party of my great grandmother, Phi Wilcox Comer, at the age of nine in 1953. She was living in Elma, Wash., with her son, Walter, age 77, who was her caregiver. Stories of her and husband William, homesteading in the very northeast prairies of Montana in the early 1900s, fascinated me.

Phi's youngest son, Clayton, was born in 1899. When he wrote a book about his teenage years in Comertown, Mont., my inquisitive fires were further lit, but it wasn't until 2018 that I had the time to visit Comertown. My "golf wife" of 45 years and fellow pharmacist, Rick Sahli, and I took an Amtrak train to Williston, N.D., to play in his in-laws' charity golf tournament. We then traveled to Plentywood, Mont., to meet people who had lived in Comertown, or had relatives who did.

When we arrived at the Sheridan Count museum, we received a royal greeting from curator Pat Tange and a special hug from 98-year-old Evedine Lane, who regaled me with stories of Phi Comer and Comertown. She instantly became my new Montana girlfriend. Phi had been Evedine's teacher and was responsible for suggesting her name after a dispute between her parents about what her name should be — Eva or Dina. Phi dramatically announced her name would be Evedine!

After many years answering questions from friends and colleagues about our family's adventures, I was encouraged to have a book written about the time travel from Comertown to Cook Solutions Group. And, since the conveyance of history is critical, I wanted to leave these stories for our grandsons and their heirs.

I hope our story serves as motivation for all who have faced challenges through their lives. Without family, people start their lives in a significant deficit. No matter how challenging one's family life is, one must not assume the victim role and succumb to the bigotry of low expectations.

I was fortunate to have two grandfathers and a grandmother — Clayton Comer and Vern and Eunice Graves — who played a significant role in my life and filled several needed gaps. As with many families, my grandparents and parents struggled greatly through World Wars I and II and the Great Depression but survived through great perseverance, which was passed on to me.

If one marries above his station, he is truly blessed. My wife of 55 years, Vicki, has been the rock of our family. Without Vicki, none of our successes, through many struggles, would have been possible. As Jerry Maguire said in the move, Vicki completes me!

Vicki and I were blessed by two daughters, Wendy and Molly, and later with Brian Cook, who joined our family when he was a sophomore in high school. My hope is that Brian's story will serve as a motivational force for many youngsters whose childhood has its rocky moments. Much can be done with hard work and determination.

Much can be learned from history, in some cases, so that it may not be repeated. I hope the generations that follow mine and Vicki's will expand on the lessons learned and will achieve a level of self-actualization.

This book has offered many life lessons, the most important among them:

- Find a way to thrive in chaos (Tom Peters)
- Beware of the soft bigotry of low expectations (President George W. Bush)
- Never let yourself become a victim (Lynne Forrest — Victim Triangle)

FROSTY'S NO SNOWMAN

- Sometimes it's the people no on imagines anything of who do the things no one can imagine (Movie: The Imitation Game)
- Be all you can be (U.S. Army)
- Practice, and enjoy, random acts of kindness (Anne Herbert)
- Treat others as you would like others to treat you (The Golden Rule)!

Frosty Comer

Replica of an early 1900's country store

Replica of an inside of an early 1900's home.

Replica of a cattle branding site.

CHAPTER 1

THE GHOSTS OF COMERTOWN

Mother Nature played us a nice little trick as we flew into Williston, N.D., on a mission to revisit history.

The thermometer tickled 60 degrees on a Friday in late October 2022 in the northeastern corner of Montana, the location of the Comer family legacy. And this was after a period of light snowfall only three days before.

"We're lucky," said Frosty Comer, who knows good fortune when he sees it. "The weather gods were with us."

Frosty's great-grandparents, William and Phi Comer, homesteaded in an area of Sheridan County that would come to be called "Comertown" in 1913.

So, as we embarked on the project of writing the book "Frosty's No Snowman," Frosty and I made a visit to the place where it all began. As we surveyed the desolate region that was once hopping with activity, you could feel the presence of the ghosts of Comertown welcoming us to their final resting place.

❄

Relatively late in life, William Walter Comer and wife Phi chose to move from Taylors Falls, Minn., to the wide-open spaces of eastern Montana. The Comers homesteaded on property about 15 miles south of the Canadian border and five miles from the western boundary to North Dakota. Soon the Comers had plenty of company, and a town being named in their honor.

Phi Lovina Wilcox, born in 1852 in New York, moved with her family to Minnesota at age six. For several years, Phi — about five feet tall and weighing less than 100 pounds but with a strong presence — taught school in the Taylors Falls area. In 1876, she married William Comer, 5-8 and 170, who was two years older. They were to have four boys — Walter, Carl, Percival and Clayton.

Early in their marriage, the Comers traded their interest in a hardware store for a farm in the Palmdale area. For many years, they eked out a living on the 137-acre farm. In 1907, , William and Phi sold their farm for what was then considered a king's ransom of $8,000. They moved to the house of William's grandfather in Taylors Falls. Then in 1910, the Comers — William now 60 years old and Phi 58 — made a bigger move.

During that time, government lands in eastern Montana were being opened for homesteading. William and Percival unloaded their livestock and drove the herd there with the intention of finding a place to live. They landed on the spot that became Comertown. The area, Clayton Comer writes in a 1978 diary, "was almost uninhabited when the Comers arrived. One could look as far as the eye could see only prairie covered with native grass. There were no roads or trails. There were a few squatters scattered over the miles of virgin land."

A year later, Phi and Clayton joined William and Percival, finding them living on a lot with only a tent and small shack. The Comers soon built a home and homesteaded 320 acres of land. Percival homesteaded 320 acres nearby. Through the next few years, many people followed suit. "By 1916, open range land was limited," Clayton writes. "Land close to the town was completely filled in."

The nearest settlements, both 60 miles away, were Ambrose, N.D., to the east and Culbertson, Mont., to the southwest. It was a five-day trip from what was to be Comertown for supplies via horse and wagon. The area, Clayton writes, was "barren to the extreme."

"There was only one tree at Lonetree Lake (of course), about three miles from the (Comer) ranch," Clayton writes. "On one of the trips to visit her sister in Minnesota, Phi brought back some dandelion plants. … they thrived."

About that time, the Great Northern Railroad built a branch line to Plentywood, Mont., 20 miles to the west of Comertown. In the fall of 1913, the Soo Line built a branch from Ambrose, N.D., to Whitetail, Mont., the line cutting right through the Comer ranch. Instead of moving, William struck a deal to get a sidetrack to load cattle, and the town was underway.

"In no time, many lots were sold," Clayton writes. "Business people started a lumber yard, hardware store, grocery store, meat market, blacksmith shop, livery stable, grain elevators, pool hall, saloon, hotel and restaurant."

In 1915, the U.S. Postal Service established a post office in the town. Initially the Soo Line called the town "Comer," but the USPS ruled that it was too similar to "Conner, Mont." The budding postmaster, W.R. Vezina, suggested "Comertown," and it was to be.

At age 16, Clayton Comer was hired as assistant postmaster, making "between $15 and $18 every three months." Vezina wound up spending much of his time in nearby Dooley, so Comer operated the post office until enlisting in the Army in 1917.

Phi enjoyed cooking "for loads of people who would drop by at mealtime," Clayton writes. Hence, she became known as "Aunt Phi" to the locals. William donated several town lots on which, with the aid of donations and labor provided by local business people and ranchers, a community social hall was built. Every weekend there were public dances, and on Sundays church was held. Phi started a free public library and was founder of the Comertown Library Social Club. In the land surrounding the hall, a park was developed in 1926. In 1941, townspeople voted to name it "Comer Park" in honor of Phi.

The heart of the community for many years was Comertown School, home of the Coyotes. The high school was upstairs; the grade school was downstairs. Harsh winters often featured snow drifts as high as 17 feet. There were dormitories for the kids to stay in town and attend school during the winter months.

Farming went well for a while for the Comers. The year 1916 proved a bumper crop that "almost paid for all the machinery the Comers had bought for the operation," Clayton writes. From 1917-23, however, due to drought, "grasshoppers and a chinook wind at the wrong time would cook the kernels of small grain, and they seldom harvested the seed they planted."

By 1923, the machinery was worn out and the land became mortgaged. The Comers sold leftover items and moved to Elma, Wash., where Phi had electricity and running water for the first time.

Comertown's peak came in the early years, when the population rose to nearly 2,000. By the 1920s, the town began to decline. A fire in 1921 destroyed several businesses. The droughts of the 1930s led to dust storms and made the land even more unsuitable for farming, and people began to leave for better opportunities elsewhere.

The schoolhouse that had grades K through 8 downstairs and the high school upstairs had fewer students as the years went on. The high school closed in 1953 and the grade school ended its run in 1965. The post office processed its final transaction in 1957. By the 1960s, Rostad's General Store had closed.

Ironically, during the '60s, the bountiful oil deposits in the county made the Comertown area one of the hottest drilling regions in the Williston Oil Basin. People, though, chose to settle elsewhere, usually in nearby towns such as Williston, Culbertson and Plentywood.

By the '70s, the only house left in town was pulled off its foundation and moved to a nearby ranch. The town's agricultural landmark burned to the ground in 2000.

Comertown Cemetery remains on a hill, overgrown and unattended. In 1993, the community was listed as a historic district by the National Register of Historic Places. In 2004, 200 people attended a Comertown reunion in Plentywood. The place in which they used to live and/or attend school is a ghost town now.

❄

The Comer/Eggers expedition flew from Portland to Williston through Minneapolis, the most direct flight possible to where we were headed. Williston is an hour and five minutes' drive from Plentywood, the closest town to where Comertown once was.

Williston's population is 29,000, making it the sixth-largest city in North Dakota. The population doubled between 2010 and 2020, due largely to the North Dakota oil boom. Located at the confluence of the Yellowstone and Missouri rivers, Williston's climate is extreme. In the winters, the temperature drops below zero on the average of 39 days a year. It averages seven days at 20-below or lower.

Plentywood is a town of 1,600, down from almost 2,500 in 1980. The town is 20 miles southwest of where Comertown once was along Montana Highway 5.

The drive from Williston to Plentywood along U.S. Route 2 is a bucolic scene out of a Norman Rockwell painting. Very few houses or signs of much civilization. It's a hazy sunny day, with patches of white stuff visible alongside the roads after light snowfall earlier in the week.

FROSTY'S NO SNOWMAN

There is flat land with no mountains and hardly a hill, but the air is clear and the mostly private land a vast display of rural Americana. We pass oil fields; many pumps are active.

We move onto Highway 85 West. The growing season is over, but we pass fields where hay, wheat and barley are cultivated in the spring and summer. Ranch houses and barns appear every so often. Patches of sage brush appear on acres of land that was once plowed using mules or oxen.

There are several switches, from Highway 85 to Highway 50, then North to Highway 516 and finally to 517. We reach Plentywood and head for the Sheridan County Museum, where a group of locals have been tipped off that Frosty Comer is coming to town. Comer had visited four years earlier to get his first look at the area in which his grandfather spent much of his childhood. He made friends who were eager to see him again.

Pat Tange, 73, is the museum curator and has arranged for a group of about 15 residents of the area to be on hand. Joe Vistler, editor of the Sheridan County News weekly, takes photos and offers some historical information. The longtime owner and CEO of the newspaper, Marvel Hellegaard, is on hand for the meeting. Retired now at 87, she is truly a marvel, with 12 children, 32 grandchildren and 36 great-grandchildren.

Vistler estimates the average age in Northeastern Montana at 55.

"We're aging out," he says.

Many of the senior citizens are gathered around a table in the museum, including Hellegaard, Richard Johnson (87) and wife Doreen (85), Otto Torgerson (80), Judy Bykonen (79), Beverley Olson (91) and Chris "Junior" Peterson (96). All of them attended school in Comertown in the 1940s and '50s.

FROSTY'S NO SNOWMAN

Frosty starts the meeting by telling everyone about the plan to write a book about Comertown and reminds them of his link through his great-grandfather and grandfather. Then we began to ask questions on what these fine folks recall about their time living and/or going to school in Comertown.

"It was a nice little town," says Bykonen, who happens to be Olson's sister. "There was a dance at the barn every weekend. We had two elementary classrooms — first through fourth grade and fifth through eighth grade. The high school was upstairs. Our grandmas cooked in the lunch room. We ate good. We walked to school every day, except in the winter when some of us stayed in dorms. We had lots of snow to play with when we were kids."

"Winter? It was easy," Richard Johnson says with a hint of a smile. "You went in the house and sat by the stove. We went with a team of horses the three miles to school."

"It could get real bad," Olson says. "Every morning in January 1950, it got to 40 below. It averaged 26 below. For a whole month, it was terrible."

"On the worst days it would get to 40 degrees below," Torgerson says. "You'd step outside and crush the snow and it would just echo. The county had two bulldozers trying to get into Comertown to keep the roads open."

As the 1940s hit the '50s, good jobs were increasingly hard to find.

"You couldn't make a living here anymore," Peterson says.

"People moved away," Hellegaard says. "The high school closed in 1953. I graduated in 1952, and I always said, the people who left tried to get along without me but they couldn't."

"They sold whisky here during prohibition," Torgerson says. "Anything you could steal and sell was OK."

FROSTY'S NO SNOWMAN

❄

Tange joins us for the 20-minute drive to Comertown. The first half runs us east on Highway 5; then we turn left on a gravel road that takes us to a place of near-forgotten history. Over the flat prairie, you can see the horizon in every direction. There are crop fields and acres of land lying fallow as far as an eye can see. This is indeed the middle of nowhere.

We do a circle and see Comertown and Phi roads, the latter named after Frosty's great-grandma. There are abandoned railroad tracks and the cemetery, where spirits surely notice our presence. There are a half-dozen dilapidated barns and farmhouses and an abandoned tractor Pat believes could be 100 years old — a potential addition to the museum. There is actually one new house surrounded by trees, which Pat believes was built by someone for use during hunting months. "But he doesn't live here," Pat says.

Well, then. Comertown's current population is zero. This is the definition of a ghost town. It must look very much as it did more than a century ago when the Comers first came upon the site. And given the land and weather, it stands a good chance to stay that way.

Still, it's an important piece of property to Frosty, who proudly holds deeds to three lots willed to him by his grandfather. Ancestors laid the foundation that following generations built into something very good. We'll talk more about that in the chapters ahead.

Hydrogen filled balloon in hanger prepared for deployment.

Front view of the Famous German Fokker

ttack by enemy plane on the Fourth Company Balloon. Note parachutes descending and the nti-aircraft shells bursting in the air. In the lower left hand corner can be seen the smoke from a alloon burnt by the same enemy plane just before the attack on the Fourth Company Balloon.

Bill Comer maintaining his ambulance in France, 1944.

Bill Comer, Hill Military Academy Graduation, Portland, OR, 1940.

Connie Comer, Marine Corps, 1943.

Clayton, Walter and Phi Comer with Frosty in Elma, WA, 1944.

Frosty Comer, 1946

Vicki Leininger, 1948

Bill "Captain Willie" Comer, KBCH, Oceanlake, OR, 1957

Eunice & Vern Graves, Portland, OR, 1950.

Plentywood/Comertown greeting party, Sheridan County Museum, 2018

Frosty with Evadine Lane, age 98, 2018

Pat Tange, Curator, Sheridan County Museum, Plentywood, MT 2022.

Comertown Post Office, 1915.

Frosty Comer at Comertown monument, 2018.

Comertown Cemetery, 2018.

Frosty Comer on antique harvester, Comertown, MT, 2022.

Comertown home, 2018.

Kerry Eggers interviewing past Comertown citizens and relatives, Plentywood, MT, 2022.

Frosty, Connie, Kim & Casey Comer, Christmas 1958, Oceanlake, OR.

Bill Comer, KPOJ all-night radio show at the Hoyt Hotel, Portland, OR, 1964.

Clayton Snow Comer, 1978

CHAPTER 2

Bringing up Frosty

Clayton Comer made good use of his time in the Army in World War I. The youngest of four boys to William and Phi Comer was stationed in France, where he served for two years fighting the Germans with the Army Balloon Corps.

The balloons were large dirigibles filled with hydrogen, powered by engines and steered with propellers. Given their gargantuan size, they moved slowly, which meant they could hover for a long period of time over both land and sea.

Rising to altitudes of between 1,200 and 1,800 feet, they could carry a larger crew of balloon observers and their equipment, machine guns and at least two tons of bombs. So some dirigibles, particularly those called "Zeppelins," became weapons. Their main mission, though, was to document the landscape during reconnaissance. This proved invaluable, the observers sighting thousands of instances of enemy plans, infantry and artillery fire. Many members of the balloon corps would stay in the air 12 hours at a time, spotting.

Figures from the National WWI Museum and Memorial show there were 35 American balloon companies in France during WWI. They ascended nearly 6,000 times, adding up to more than 6,800 hours in the air. Their balloons were attacked 89 times; 35 burned, 12 were shot down by enemy fire and one floated into enemy lines.

The large size of the balloons made them easy targets for airplanes. German snipers and German Fokker Airplanes ("Red Baron" mono-planes) were known to shoot at balloons; on direct hit, they exploded. There are pictures of U.S. soldiers parachuting out and Germans shooting at them.

Once discharged in 1919, Clayton returned to the States. He married Mayme McKay in 1921 in Bismarck, N.D. A son, William Blair Comer, was born in 1922. He would be known as "Bill" throughout his life. The Comers moved to Tacoma, Wash., in the middle '30s.

Clayton worked for McKesson, a major wholesaler for pharmacies. In the late 1930s, Clayton and a friend, Wayne Hanby, started their own wholesale business, calling it "Comer and Hanby." It provided everything a retail pharmacy would sell, including over-the-counter drugs, gifts, first-aid supplies, and perfumes. Hanby filled orders in the office. Comer drove his 1936 DeSoto around the Northwest, calling on local pharmacies. There were no chain drugstores in those days. When Clayton came to a town where a pharmacy owner had either passed away or retired, and if it made financial sense, he would buy it.

"He was a '40s version of a venture capitalist," says Clayton's grandson, Frosty Comer. "But he was very magnanimous about it. He always offered a fair deal."

Clayton would begin as 100 percent owner of the retail store. After a period of time, to be determined by the success of the pharmacist he had hired, Clayton would sell as much as 90 percent of it to the pharmacist.

"He would always keep 10 percent to have his fingers in it, but not a controlling interest," Frosty says. "He was always there for advice and support."

FROSTY'S NO SNOWMAN

One of those whom Clayton worked with was Vern Patrick, who succeeded him as majority owner of Cent-Wise Drugs in Redmond, Ore. Clayton and Patrick met at a Pocatello, Ida., retail pharmacy in the early '40s, and when Clayton purchased Cent-Wise in Redmond in 1948, he hired Patrick to run the pharmacy. A few years later, Clayton sold 90 percent of the business to Patrick, and they formed a partnership to invest in other pharmacies in the Northwest.

In the heyday of Cent-Wise Drugs, there were locations in Oregon in east Portland, Cedar Hills, Albany, Redmond, Springfield and two in Lebanon. The other store was in Forks, Wash.

When Clayton died in 1982, all of his ownership (generally 10 percent) in any remaining Cent-Wise stores went to the majority owner and not to his estate. Patrick ran the Redmond pharmacy until it closed in 1992.

"Clayton was the patriarch of Cent-Wise drugstores," Frosty says. "He would provide the pharmacy owner with products through Comer and Hanby — over-the-counter drugs, but also toys, perfume, knick knacks, gifts, stationery, figurines, etc. Those were placed in the front end of the store and helped the pharmacies make money.

"One of the great things my grandfather taught me was to empower folks by allowing them ownership while still keeping a percentage to maintain the partnership relationship."

Frosty, in fact, used that philosophy in helping one of his daughters, Molly Angelo and Brian Cook, start a business. We'll get to that later in the book.

Clayton Comer stayed in the pharmacy wholesale business for about 25 years. Mayme, Clayton's first wife, struggled with alcoholism, and they divorced in 1956. Clayton lived for a short while in Des Moines, Wash., but then he met Marjorie Denny from Fresno, Calif. They were married in 1958 and moved to Fresno.

"Grandpa Clayton sold mutual funds for Waddell and Reed for several years in Fresno, and at one point got an award as one of the top sales reps in the country," Frosty says. "Later, he helped fund a German auto parts store and a shoe store. He worked until his mid- '70s. He was never one to sit still. He liked to be active. He liked to be a mentor.

"He was a salesman. He could sell you your laptop while you're typing on it. There wasn't anything he couldn't sell. The way he sold it, you just wanted to buy it from him. He connected with people."

Frosty got to know Clayton well into his adulthood.

"He was fun," Frosty says. "He'd sit and smoke his cigars, tell stories and taught me how to play cribbage. The only thing he didn't talk about was his military career. When I was stationed with the Army's 45th Field Hospital in Italy from 1969-72, he came over and visited us twice. Instead of seeing the sights, he'd rather spend time with us on the base or eating in the PX."

❄

Clayton and Mayme Comer lived in Tacoma, but they sent their son Bill to Hill Military Academy in Portland for high school. Attending Grant High School was Connie Graves, who was born and raised in Portland. Bill and Connie graduated from high school in 1940. After a two-year courtship, they were married in October 1942.

"Mom was a gorgeous woman," Frosty says. "She could have been a model. She was very smart and talented. She attended Willamette University for one year and really wanted to finish college, but World War II interrupted that."

Bill joined the Coast Guard at the beginning of the War, but then enlisted in the Army. Bill was initially stationed in Fort Lewis, Wash. After they married, they decided to have Connie enlist in the Marines, so they could be together in Virginia. Bill was stationed in Norfolk, Connie in Quantico.

"She was what they called, in the Marine Corps, a 'BAM' — a broad-assed Marine," jokes Frosty about his mother. "That's the way it was back then."

Careful what you wish for. Shortly after they got to Virginia, Bill was shipped back to Fort Lewis. Before he left, they went into scramble mode.

"She got pregnant with me," Frosty says. "He got his orders to go back to Fort Lewis, they made quick whoopee and presto!"

Bill left Fort Lewis, Wash., after basic training on Oct. 6, 1943. He arrived via train at Camp Kilmer, N.J. and boarded a ship that left the New York harbor on Oct. 21.

Bill wrote a diary that began with his trip overseas until he was discharged about two months after the war ended. "Very interesting to read," Frosty says. "It's day after day after day of boredom, and then all of a sudden, chaos."

Comer was a medic/ambulance driver in England and France. He spent about a year in England, then was transferred to Paris with his unit in November 1944. He was in France for about a year and a half, earning his honorable discharge and left the military as a corporal.

Meanwhile, William Foster Comer was born on March 13, 1944. The middle name comes from the maiden name of his grandmother Eunice. "Frosty," a nickname for Foster, came quickly. Bill found out about Frosty's birth from a Red Cross telegram shortly after his son was born. By that time, Bill was already referring to him as "Frosty" in his diary.

Frosty was born in Tacoma. His mother was living there with her sister, Virginia, with Bill overseas. By the time Bill returned home after his honorable discharge, Frosty was 2 1/2.

"When Dad left the military, he wasn't used to having people around to care for," Frosty says. "He had to worry about staying alive."

The Comers set up house at the Sandycrest Terrace apartments in Northeast Portland. One night soon after he got home, Bill took Frosty on a walk across Sandy Boulevard on a mission.

"He was going to get some takeout at the Coon Chicken Inn, a name that would be very inappropriate today," Frosty says. "When he got home, Mom asked, 'Where's Frosty?' He had left me there at the restaurant. He had never had a kid around before."

Frosty was close to his mother. He wasn't sure about his relationship with his father.

"Having been in the military, it is easier for me to understand why Dad wasn't the dad I wanted him to be," Frosty says. "Bill's dad was always on the road. His mom was an alcoholic. He would come home to either an empty house or to Mayme passed out. When it came time to be a parent, all he knew was to work his ass off. So my mom was the mother, and also the father. When I was eight or nine, I broke one of her fingers playing catch with a baseball."

Bill worked at a bank for a year, earning $100 a month. Then he got an offer to work for Clayton. A branch of Comer and Hanby was opened in Portland, and Bill became its sales representative.

"But in that job, you have to go on the road to sell," Frosty says. "Could he sell? Yes. But he hated it. He was away again by himself."

Home often enough, however, to provide Frosty with a sibling. Kathleen, called Casey, was born on Nov. 5, 1947. Through his childhood, Frosty served as protector.

"It was, 'Don't mess with my sister,'" Frosty says. "We got along well. She wasn't the most athletic, but she loved sports. We had some really fun times together. I hated snakes. Casey knew it. One time she grabbed a garter snake in the yard and whirled it around her head and chased me into the house.

"She was always trying to keep up with me. One time she fell off the jungle gym and broke her arm. She was a little monkey like I was. Casey would never take her vitamins. She'd pretend to take them and put them into my dresser drawer. Then she'd tell on me. It took a while for Mom to realize that she was pulling a prank."

Connie's parents, Vern and Eunice Graves, lived in Portland and were important figures in Frosty's life.

Vern — Frosty called him "Gramps" — was the manager of Miller's Department Store in the Hollywood district of Northeast Portland.

"At Christmas, he would be Santa at the Hollywood Theater," Frosty says. "Eunice was the sweetest lady, but twice she backed the car out of the garage without opening the door. They lived on a hill across the street from Rose City Grade School. It was a great place for sledding in the wintertime. They'd always have something for us to do. Many times, Casey and I would go over there and my mother's sister would come down with her two kids."

Bill Comer started a used car shop on Northeast Broadway, calling it "Big-Hearted Bill's Used Cars on Broadway."

"That lasted a year or two," Frosty says. "At one point, he got robbed. They got into his office and stole some keys and a car. Dad was a lot like his father. He was really good with folks. If anything, he trusted them too much."

Frosty and Casey lived with their maternal grandparents for part of a year when their parents went to New York City. Bill was training to work with his father's Comer and Hanby business. Frosty would attend three different grade schools during the 1950-51 academic year. When Bill and Connie returned they purchased a house at 36th and Northeast Going, paid for it through the GI Bill with help from both sets of grandparents.

"My parents were just trying to survive, living day to day, paycheck to paycheck," Frosty says. "Out of this chaos, they became creative and learned how to get by on what they had and with what their family could help them. Their parents had lived through the Depression and World Wars I and II. Nothing went to waste. It wasn't altruistic; it was out of necessity. My grandparents saved coffee grounds until there wasn't anything left of them."

Frosty didn't feel poor. There was no television set, so he would play an "over the line" baseball game with friends in the neighborhood streets for hours. There was a basketball hoop in the Comers' driveway. "I told myself I couldn't go to dinner until I made 10 straight free throws," he says.

"We had a cherry tree in the backyard," Frosty says. "I could climb anything. Casey and I would go to the grocery store three blocks away and buy penny candy."

But life at home was not easy. His father was on the road often for his job.

"Our lives were in chaos," Frosty says. "Mom was totally consumed. Dad was not there. I had nobody to help me with homework. I had to learn how to learn. Because of our grandparents, we were able to hold it together financially, and Mom's parents were there a lot. Without them and Clayton, our family may not have survived."

In 1953, Bill Comer came down with spinal polio. He spent 18 months at the Veterans Administration hospital in Portland.

"Dad's left leg was paralyzed, and when he came out of the VA hospital it was two inches shorter than his right," Frosty says. "He ended up getting hooked on Tylenol with codeine while in the VA. Eventually he broke the addiction. Walking was painful, but he was able to tolerate it. He was very lucky to be alive, or to not be in an iron lung."

To make matters more complicated, Connie was pregnant with twins. Daughters Connie and Kimberly were born May 13, 1954.

"Now Dad had four kids and no college education," Frosty says. "We were lucky our grandparents helped. There were no food stamps or welfare in those days. There might have been a little VA benefit, but no housing allowance. Back then, it was up to families to take care of families."

Connie's parents found the means to hire a maid to help with household duties until Bill returned home.

"It was my first exposure to an African American, and she was amazing," Frosty says. "She was a big help. She cooked, cleaned, and helped us when Casey and I got home from school."

After his release from the hospital, the VA paid for Bill to attend radio licensing school. He received his third-class radio operator's license and worked for seven days at a Portland radio station before getting fired.

❄

Frosty attended Kennedy Grade School through fifth grade. The kids and teachers called him "Billy" for a while.

"When friends would come to our home to play, they quickly started calling me 'Frosty,' " he says. "I gave up Billy when we moved to Oceanlake and was called Frosty from then on."

Frosty wasn't a good student at Kennedy.

"I had to learn how to go to school," he says. "We had good teachers. I remember getting into trouble doing stupid things, but I don't remember being all that sad about it. I was just a kid who didn't have a lot of direction."

FROSTY'S NO SNOWMAN

The Comers moved to Oceanlake — now part of Lincoln City — when Frosty was in sixth grade in 1955.

Bill Comer was hired as a disc jockey at KBCH Radio in Oceanlake. The Comers, now six strong, rented a house in Roads End for the summer. At the end of the summer, they moved to a place on the east end of Devils Lake. And soon thereafter, Bill was fired. He quickly got a job writing for the News-Guard newspaper for three months.

"Dad was scrambling to stay employed," Frosty says. "So finally Clayton tells him, 'Enough of this. I'll help you buy one-third of KBCH.' Dad went back to work there, and he thrived. He had this great personality. He had a great voice. He understood what it meant to connect with the community."

A November kidney infection sidelined Frosty from school for 2 1/2 months that was diagnosed by Dr. Peabody, who would make weekly house visits to administer intramuscular procaine penicillin injections. They would be so painful, Frosty says, that he couldn't walk for two days. Peabody then prescribed daily oral penicillin for the following 5 years. After his recovery, Frosty jumped into activities in his new environment. He returned in time to play Little League baseball, as a second baseman and pitcher. In the eighth grade, he earned enough money through odd jobs to buy a 10-foot wooden rowboat.

"I had a friend come over one day," Frosty says. "I decided I was John Paul Jones and was going to take him to his home in Delake, the west end of Devils Lake, 4 ½ miles away, in the rowboat. I got him back to the D River and had to row back home myself. The wind came up. It was all I could do to keep from getting blown back in the wrong direction. I was two hours overdue. Luckily, somebody saw me struggling and came out in their motor boat and towed me back to my house."

Frosty says he would entertain himself by hitting rocks into Devils Lake with a wood bat.

"I'd have wiffle-ball games with my sisters," he says. "I was a built-in babysitter for my folks."

By the time Frosty reached high school, his father had somehow found the money to buy a 16-foot ski boat.

"We would go to Kenny Morgan's house on the lake, and all the high school kids would come and we would water ski all day long in the summer," Frosty says. "The Morgans had a boat with a 90-horse Mercury engine, and it could pull six skiers. I got good enough where I could slalom ski with a jump start off the dock. When I was done, I would ski up to the shore and walk out of my skis. It was a great life for us kids, growing up on Devils Lake."

The Comers were paying only $50 monthly rent for the three-story house on two acres right on the lake, thanks to the generosity of the owners, Jess and Nettie Utter.

"It was a really cool house, with an elevator and a fireplace in the master bedroom," Frosty says. "They let us live there for almost nothing. Nettie and Jess became like an aunt and uncle to our family."

❄

Times were a-changing in America, and by Frosty's freshman year at Taft High in 1958, a new genre of music had arrived.

"All the kids loved rock and roll," he says. "We could listen to it on KEX in Portland on our radios at certain times of the day. And we had 45 rpm records. There was Elvis, Jerry Lee Lewis, Little Richard. Dad worked at KBCH — we joked it stood for 'Keep Bill Comer Happy' — so he was in the music scene.

"Dad's biggest flaw was he didn't think rock and roll would make it. We had an argument about it. Dad said rock and roll will never last. I said, 'I will guarantee you it will last.' We made a bet my freshman year. If it was still popular by the time I graduated, I would get to have one hour on KBCH to play just rock and roll. I won the bet, of course, but we moved back to Portland at the start of my junior year."

Frosty's mother got into the act with a "ladies talk show" on KBCH that she hosted remotely from the master bedroom of the Comer home.

"One day, Mom was on the air talking about the latest recipes, and in the background you could hear Connie, one of the twins who was now 4 years old, yell 'Mommy!' " Frosty says. "Mom tried to ignore it. Then it's, 'Mommy, come wipe my bottom on live radio!' And Mom says, 'Yes, Connie, I'll be there in a minute.' It was Mayberry RFD.

"But that's what's so great about small-town America. There was a symbiotic relationship in the town. You bought everything in town or else. Buy a car in Salem or Portland and you would be ostracized. There was loyalty and a lot of giving just to survive. Everyone called the miles between Otis to Depoe Bay the '20 Miracle Miles,' since the joke was it was a miracle to survive economically through the winter months, just like in Comertown, Mont. Because of his experience with polio, Dad put on an annual 24-hour radiothon for the March of Dimes at the local theater. People attended throughout the 24 hours and would call in with pledges and auction items for donations. It was one of the best March of Dimes fundraising events in Oregon at that time."

Frosty entered Taft High as a 5-6, 130-pound freshman.

"Early in the school year, I was walking down the hall and, all of a sudden, these juniors and seniors had me surrounded and started pushing me," he says. "Nobody swung at me, but I was getting pissed about being bullied. I reached out and cold-cocked this one guy in the jaw. He fell and, all of a sudden, everybody stepped back, and it was over. They left me alone after that and I became part of the group."

Frosty was a varsity second baseman as a freshman and sophomore at Taft. His grades were improving.

"I was happy living there," he says, "and then Dad takes an offer from KEX to work in their newsroom."

Bill sold KBCH and moved the family back to Portland, but there was a detour to Roseburg in the summer of '60. He worked as a reporter and disc jockey for KQEN radio. Frosty enjoyed playing for the Roseburg American Legion baseball team that summer. Finally, the job opened at KEX and the Comers were in Portland, living in a house in Wilson Heights.

Frosty entered his junior year at Wilson High School, intimidated by the size of the student body. Taft high school had under 400 students but his junior class at Wilson high school had over 400 students with a total high school population of over 2,000, larger than the town of Oceanlake!

"What turned the table was I was decent at sports," he says.

At first, he focused on baseball. He made the junior varsity as a junior and was starting second baseman for the varsity as a senior.

"I had good coaching from Bob Webster, and we had a really good team," Frosty recalls. "My senior year, we went 18-3 and tied with Madison, which was led by pitcher Rick Wise, for the city championship."

Wise would go on to win 188 games as a pitcher in 18 major-league seasons.

"I hit over .300," Comer says. "Richie Vose was our big pitching stud, who later played in the Yankees organization. Madison beat us in the playoff game for the right to go to state. We were all in tears on the bus back to Wilson."

Frosty made the basketball varsity as "13th man" as a junior but didn't go out as a senior. Instead, he tried football despite his diminutive frame.

"I was third-string running back and second-string linebacker," he says. "I learned to love defense. They couldn't block me. I could beat them across the line. But I didn't play much in games. When I did, it was on defense.

"Sports was an avenue to toughen you up, teach you discipline, responsibility and accountability and helped you develop a network of friends. My senior year, we had 12 sports teams at Wilson and nine of them either won or tied for city championships. Around town, we were known as the 'country club snobby kids on the hill.' I didn't feel that way. At least, my family wasn't rich."

During those years, Bill's job as a reporter at KEX was going well.

"Some of the stuff he did was revolutionary," Frosty says. "He would not shave for a week, dress down, go down to Burnside and interview the bums. He would sleep overnight on the street with them. He did a great job."

After five years, Bill moved to KPOJ and hosted an overnight show at the Hoyt Hotel.

"He interviewed celebrities like Johnny Mathis and Mike Wallace," Frosty says. "I remember Mike saying Dad was the best interviewer — next to him."

Frosty graduated from Wilson in 1962. It was time to move on to the next part of his life. He was ready for it, and yet he wasn't.

CHAPTER 3

Along Comes Vicki

Frosty Comer's mother, Connie Graves, had attended Willamette University in Salem her freshman year, which was interrupted by WWII and her marriage to Bill Comer. Frosty was interested in the medical field, and Willamette — with an enrollment of 1,200 — seemed a good fit, at least to Bill and Connie Comer.

"A lot of my friends were going to Oregon State or Oregon, but my parents thought a smaller school would be better for me," Frosty says.

Wilson High had offered a unique medical preceptorship for its students, allowing them to shadow a physician.

"I got an exceptional doctor, Dr. Douglas Day, a physician/surgeon, for a medical experience program my senior year," Frosty says. "He was very good with patients. I would get a call from him. 'Frosty, I've got a house call to make at 10 tonight. I'll pick you up.'

"We'd go to the patients' home. One time I got to scrub down and assist in a surgery. The patient was a 38-year-old Asian who was undergoing a tonsillectomy. I was like a surgical nurse. I had to scrub down. I suctioned the blood from his throat so the doctor could see to remove it. Boy, was it bloody. ... and I watched during the delivery of a baby. For a high school kid, this was some amazing stuff."

Mind you, this was the early 1960's.

"Tort law was much different in those days, and this was a formal student/preceptor program," Frosty says. "Dr. Day was very good and careful. He took me on home visits at all hours of the day and night. It was a great introduction into how to treat and talk to patients under stress."

Frosty kept in touch with Day for several years.

"He became a mentor and source of encouragement," Frosty says. "My goal had been to be a pediatrician. That resulted from having younger sisters, especially the twins, because I ended up taking care of them a lot. I related to kids well. When I realized I wasn't going to make it to medical school, I felt like I really let Dr. Day, my parents, and grandparents down."

Frosty enrolled at Willamette for fall term in 1962. His major was biology. He lived in a dormitory, Baxter Hall, and joined a fraternity, Sigma Chi.

"I had a lot of fun being away from home for the first time," Frosty says. "I didn't live in the house as a freshman. I really wasn't ready. But I had a lot of fun and made some good friends."

Frosty made the varsity baseball team as a freshman second baseman.

"I played some, but was mostly on the bench," he says.

Frosty says he experienced racism for the first time.

"I had a good friend, Richard Payne, a black kid, a good athlete, a great guy," he says. "We were in the dorm together. We went through Rush together. Evidently, Sigma Chi had to send a picture of the pledges to the home office in Atlanta. When it came time, I was told by the brothers that they would like to pledge him, but it would never pass nationally. It wasn't fair. He wound up pledging Phi Delta Theta. It was our loss."

Frosty was no more than an average student at Willamette. He struggled with his studies.

"My classes included biology, chemistry, physics, analytical geometry and calculus, German and history of Christianity," he says. "It was a load for anybody. I was up against a lot of 4-pointer classmates."

Frosty seemed more successful at extracurricular activities.

"I wasn't a partier, and I didn't drink much in college," he says. "I didn't drink at all in high school. Willamette was a very restrictive Methodist school. We had to attend chapel. But I wasn't a wallflower."

Frosty's nickname at Willamette was "The Fly."

"I could climb almost anything," he says.

It came in handy during one episode of high jinks.

"One time a bunch of upperclassmen had a kegger in a barn off campus," Frosty says. "They wanted us to get some food for the party from Saga Food Service at Baxter Hall. My friend, who worked for Saga, asked for my help. He left a second-story window unlocked. I climbed up the south end of the dorm, crawled into the window, unlocked the door and let my classmate go into the freezer and deduct the inventory of steaks we would have eaten the next night. Then I closed the window and I climbed back down. We did not consider this stealing because we had already paid for the food service at the beginning of the semester. Fortunately, I didn't get caught.

"Guys from frats and dorms would sometimes head across the campus and storm the female dorms for a panty raid. Everybody wore masks to hide their identity. Unfortunately, my roommate, Bud Adams, was 6-6 and stood out in the crowd. He got identified and got kicked out of school.

"We had major water balloon fights around the dorms during the spring. It was in good fun, but a couple of times the school security called the Salem police. When they came, students atop the roofs nailed them with water balloons from above. Nobody ever got caught. Nobody got hurt. It was good times."

Frosty was on the varsity wrestling team as a sophomore, cutting to 123 pounds.

"All I could do that season was eat, sleep and wrestle," he says. "It sucked all the energy out of me. I didn't miss class, but my test scores were horrible.

"What I learned was, don't overestimate. You can't just jump in and do something you've not trained for. You think you're good enough, but when the rubber meets the road, you'll find your limitations quickly. I was stupid enough to think I could wrestle and still maintain grades good enough to get into med school. But with a 1.75 GPA halfway through my sophomore fall semester, my folks had a 'come-to-Jesus' talk with me about getting serious about college."

During his sophomore year, Frosty got a call that his parents were getting a divorce after 22 years of marriage. He wasn't surprised. The main issue, he felt, was money. He remembered being a young boy and hearing arguments.

"How are we going to put food on the table?" Frosty recalls them asking. "There was always that financial stress. It wasn't a good thing for my sisters, who were still at home, but it just wasn't going to work."

Frosty lived at the Sigma Chi house during his sophomore and junior years, serving as house secretary as a junior. After his junior year, his cumulative grade-point average improved to a 2.4.

"It was time to get serious after I had the meeting with my folks and grandparents," he says. "Vietnam was heating up. It became obvious I wasn't going to get into med school."

Bill Comer would marry twice more. He left KPOJ and moved to Guam, where he ran a food cart operation. He returned to Oregon, started a PR firm, managed a restaurant in Woodburn and finally worked as a maître d' at the Kon Tiki Lounge in downtown Portland. Bill died at 60 of heart complications in 1982.

"He bounced around from job to job throughout his adult life," Frosty says. "That's what happens when you don't get an education. That's why he did everything he possibly could to help all four of his kids graduate from college."

Connie married Tom Bowen, whom she had known as far back as grade school. She was 89 when she died as the result of a fall in 2012.

❄

Before he entered Willamette, Frosty attended a freshman orientation camp at Silver Creek Falls east of Salem. The summer before his junior year, he served as its co-chairman.

"That had been one of my goals since I had attended it," Frosty says. "It was really beneficial. I learned how to plan and how to execute a major project. You had accountability and responsibility and mentoring duties. My secretary job at the fraternity helped in that regard, too.

"Looking back on my time at Willamette, I had a lot of challenges and failures, but one thing the fraternities and sports taught me, don't overestimate your abilities. My junior year, my grades were getting better. I wasn't the pariah in the biology class anymore."

In the summer of 1965, Frosty transferred to Oregon State. His grandfather, Clayton Comer, helped him out financially.

"To earn money, I ironed shirts for other students and worked in the cafeterias at Wilson and McNary dorms," he says. "I decided not to rejoin the Sigma Chi fraternity at Oregon State. I had made up my mind I wasn't going to participate in an organization that wouldn't accept people of color."

Frosty lived in Wilson Hall his first year at OSU. The resident assistant was Bill Pigeon, who was also in pharmacy college with Frosty.

"I took a ton of hours that year — 21, 22 and 21 hours, both biology and pharmacy classes," he says.

Frosty was a year away from a biology degree. He didn't want to give that up.

"I basically double-majored to finish my final year of biology requirements so that I could complete my degree at Willamette," he says. Frosty wasn't able to walk with his classmates during commencement ceremonies in May 1966 because Willamette was on semesters and Oregon State was on the quarter system. He got his Bachelor of Arts in biology in June.

In the summer of 1965, to get caught up so he could go into the junior class of the OSU pharmacy school, he took classes such as pharmaceutical calculations, inorganic and organic pharmaceutical chemistry. On his first test in pharmaceutical calculations, he got a D.

"Boy, was that a slap in the face," he says. "I was really good in math, but I was sloppy. I wasn't focused."

Frosty singles out Harriet Sisson and Dr. Robert Dorge as favorite teachers during his time at Oregon State.

"Harriet Sisson made you appreciate the need to focus and be 100 percent accurate in pharmacy," he says. "She emphasized that if you screw up with a simple decimal point you can kill people. She was no-nonsense. Dr. Dorge was such a gentleman and so good with students. I couldn't have had two better professors."

At Oregon State, the format was four 12-week quarters. "I much preferred the shorter blocks of studies," says Frosty, who wound up getting a 4.0 GPA during each of his final two years at OSU, in grad school in 1973-74 and in residence in 1974-75. "Fear does wonders," he says.

During Frosty's senior year in college but his first year at Oregon State, he took human anatomy in an auditorium with 150 students.

Bill Pigeon was also in the class. One day, Frosty was hit by a sight to behold.

"Bouncing down the stairs came a young lady in an Army Sponsor Corps uniform," Frosty says.

It was a sophomore coed named Vicki Leininger.

"I told Bill, who was a resident assistant at a nearby dormitory to Vicki's, 'I have to find out who that is,' " Frosty says. "I was still pretty shy back then."

Vicki was a resident assistant for Buxton Hall.

"I also met her in the human anatomy lab," Frosty says. "We started chatting. She had so many boyfriends at the time."

Pigeon arranged a get-together between Weatherford and Buxton dorms and invited Frosty to come.

"Bill was a good-looking California surfer dude and was hanging out with Vicki," Frosty says. "At some point, 'The Troll' (Frosty) joined in, and that's when we started dating."

❄

In May 1966, toward the end of Frosty's first year at OSU, he got a draft notice from the Army.

"I called my dad and told him, 'I'm not going to be able to finish pharmacy school,' " Frosty says. "Dad took me to a Navy recruiting station in Portland to see if I could get a direct commission, since I had a degree from Willamette. The Naval officials just laughed since they were overwhelmed with such requests."

The Comers went to the Army and Air Force ROTC units to see

what they had to offer. Army officials said they could "guarantee" Frosty could be a pharmacy officer if he would enter the new two-year ROTC program.

Because of an overwhelming number of casualties in Vietnam, the Army needed candidates for second lieutenants. It implemented a two-year ROTC program and an eight-week basic training course during the summer of '66, which made up for the first two years of the four-year requirement.

Frosty enrolled. He attended the boot camp in July and August in Fort Knox, Ky.

"It was hot, muggy and buggy with lots of lightning at night that would light up the sky," he says. "This is where the lessons I learned at Willamette started to pay off, though I was still a wise ass. All instructors were drill sergeants or Officer Candidate School graduates — enlisted guys smart and dedicated enough to go through what they had to in order to become officers. They hated us "smart-ass college kids!". I can remember laughing in the middle of a formation and getting called out during boot camp.

"But I had a really great drill sergeant and a reasonable captain. I was two years older (22) than a lot of these guys. I had to have an attitude adjustment: 'If you're going to survive this, don't be a wise ass. Call upon the education you've got.' The academic side of it was pretty simple. We had kids from all over the country. We had guys coming in with hair down to their ass. The first place we went was to the barber shop. There were stacks of hair ankle high on the floor."

Soldiers were placed in companies, with four squads to a company and 11 soldiers to a squad. They underwent weapons training, live ammunition firing and crawling under barbwire and around pits that had explosions in them.

"At 5-6 and 135, I was one of the smaller guys, but I was strong for my size," Frosty says. "I remember going through a low-crawl obstacle course in mud that was probably a football field long. You had your M14 rifle, and you were on your back with live machine gun ammunition whizzing a few feet over your head, with tracers every fifth round. You dealt with ticks and fireflies.

"I remember sitting in the back of the barracks at night with lightning storms overhead. If you could harvest that lightning, you could power the world. We would go on 20-mile marches in the middle of the day, carrying a backpack that weighed at least 15 pounds in 90 plus degree heat and humidity. It was agony up the hills and ecstasy down them. That was the physical part. That's where I learned to drink cold beer. You had to be in shape. If you weren't in shape, you got in shape. I don't remember too many people dropping out."

Basic training included a mental component.

"There was a lot of practical academic stuff, such as night compass courses, artillery geometry, command and control leadership training, organizational structures of all the corps," Frosty says. "Also, you needed to adjust your attitude to take it seriously, since we were told what might be awaiting us overseas."

Frosty returned to Corvallis in September for his second year at Oregon State in 1966. He lived with two other students in an apartment not far from campus. It was a two-bedroom apartment. Frosty had one bedroom and the roommates shared the other.

"They were younger," Frosty says. "One was a sophomore, the other a junior. I was a fifth-year senior. I pulled rank on them. We all got along great."

Frosty took several pharmacy and ROTC classes during the 1966-67 school year.

"I also took English saddle horseback riding," he says with a grin.

"We would ride across campus to McAlexander Fieldhouse. I took six hours a quarter of ROTC. We had to drill on campus, then go to McDonald Forest for weapon training. I got straight A's in ROTC, and my pharmacy grades got better."

In one of his more challenging pharmacy, courses, pharmacognosy -- the study of plant-based medications -- He got an A with his lab partner, Bill Frenzel.

"We selected the medicinal lab assignment to determine the human biological metabolite of diazepam (Valium)," Frosty says. "We each took a 2-mg tablet of Valium, went golfing and collected our urine for 24 hours.

"Upon our return to the lab the next day, we distilled our urine and ran it through the 'thin layer chromatography process.' We then ran the needed drug identification on the results and proved it was another benzodiazepine drug called Serax, was less potent than Valium.

"While Bill and I enjoyed a day of golfing in the sun, our fellow pharmacy students were slaving away in the lab all day. The 'A' we got was 'frosting on the cake!'"

❄

Vicki Leininger was raised in North Bend, Oregon in a sports environment. Her father, Arthur "Curly" Leininger, was a well-known baseball man who coached semi-pro ball for years and served as general manager of the Coos Bay-North Bend Athletics, Oakland's Class A-short season farm team, from 1970-72. Players such as Chet Lemon, Claudell Washington and Glenn Abbott got started in "the Bay" on their way to successful major-league careers. Vicki's brother, Terry, was an outstanding three-sport athlete at North Bend High and is a member of the school's Athletic Hall of Fame. Terry went on to play baseball at the University of Oregon.

"The most wonderful man I've ever known," Vicki says of her father. "I put him on a pedestal."

Curly worked for a lumber mill, then for a printing company and finally as assessor for Coos County. Vicki's mother, Connie, worked as a dental assistant.

Vicki — renowned nationally as the only woman with a father named Curly and a husband named Frosty — was a cheerleader at North Bend High and as a freshman at Southwest Oregon Community College.

"Growing up, my mother sewed all of my clothes," Vicki says. "She made my cheerleading outfits, knitted my sweaters. She did all of that, plus she worked her job. She had innate energy. She was always there for my dad, my brother and me."

After a year at SOCC, Vicki had planned to transfer to Oregon before a discussion with brother Terry.

"Vicki, this is not the school for you," he told her. "You shouldn't go here. It's too liberal."

"He was being protective of me," Vicki says today. "So I decided to go to Oregon State instead."

Vicki arrived at Oregon State in 1965 as a PE and health major. As a junior in 1966-67, she had the occasion to meet Frosty Comer.

"Eventually, he called and asked me out," Vicki says. "His roommate dated one of my friends at Buxton, so we would double-date. I liked him because he was very friendly. We had a lot of fun together."

The relationship wasn't without minor speed bumps.

During Vicki's junior year — Frosty's second year at Oregon State — he and his roommates threw a party in their apartment. Vicki and Frosty had been dating, so she was invited to attend.

"It was April and I had horrible hay fever," Frosty recalls. "That day there were grass seeds flying all over the Willamette Valley. Everybody started coming over for the party. I'd taken an antihistamine and poured myself an ice and vodka gimlet. We hadn't yet gotten to the class of drug and alcohol interactions in pharmacy school.

"We were playing music. About 8 p.m. I decided I was going to go lay down for a little bit. I was tired. About 9 or 9:30 my roommate comes in and says Vicki's pissed. She wants to go back to the dorm. He took my car and took her home. I learned the hard way that there's a synergistic reaction between alcohol and antihistamines."

The next day, Frosty phoned Vicki to apologize.

"And I didn't listen," Vicki says. "He had to come to the door and apologize to me. He should have been paying attention to me. I thought we were together. But we made up. Not long after that, we went to a Bill Cosby concert."

❄

Frosty was reaching the point for the need to make some important decisions. One of them was his future with the military.

By the spring of '67, "I knew I didn't want to be in the service for a career, but I knew it would be a big part of my life for a few years," he says.

That summer, Frosty went to Fort Lewis for a senior ROTC summer camp, which determined where he would be placed for his last year in ROTC. There was the possibility that he would qualify to be "potentially in charge of all four years of cadets."

"I went up there with a much better attitude," Frosty says. "I was 23, going up against a lot of guys two years younger, and I already had a degree in biology (at Willamette). The academic portion of it was quite extensive. You had physical fitness tests to do, too."

With the command watching, Frosty finished first among 600 cadets in the fitness and academic tests during camp.

"Later that November, back at OSU, I led all 600 Army, Navy and Air Force ROTC cadets onto the Parker Stadium field for the opening ceremonies and national anthem before the OSU-USC football game," he says. That was the game in which Oregon State upset O.J. Simpson and the No. 1-ranked Trojans 3-0 with the governors of California, Ronald Reagan, and Oregon, Tom McCall, in attendance."

That school year, Frosty was inducted into the Scabbard and Blade ROTC honorary and also graduated as a Distinguished Military Graduate with the option to become Regular Army, which he chose to decline.

Frosty's commitment through the ROTC program was for two years of regular Army, then four years of reserve. The ROTC commitment came with a $100 monthly stipend.

"That bought my food for two years," he says. "My parents were in no position to help, so that was what I used for food. Luckily, back then, the tuition/books/room bill was a lot cheaper than today."

During the 1967-68 academic year, Frosty served as president of the Student American Pharmacy Association. He helped organize the school of pharmacy's blood drive for the university, working with the Red Cross. Nearly 1,000 students donated blood at the Red Cross set-up in the basement of the Memorial Union.

Among the three options for assignment upon graduation from ROTC, Frosty chose the Medical Service Corps. After graduation, he was commissioned as a second lieutenant.

"I wanted to serve my time, get out, come back to Oregon, find a nice community, set up a Cent-Wise pharmacy and be a small-town retail pharmacist," he says.

When Frosty returned from ROTC summer camp in August, Vicki was in a teaching program at Oregon College of Education in Monmouth. She then began her year of student teaching at Lebanon High.

Lebanon was only a 20-minute drive from Corvallis, so they were together often that fall.

To celebrate Vicki's 21st birthday on Dec. 12, 1967, she and Frosty went to a bar in Philomath with one of Frosty's pharmacy classmates, Bill Frenzel, and his wife Beryl Ann.

"Since we were graduating in six months and had no idea where or if we'd see each other after graduation, I asked her to marry me in the backseat of Bill's car," Frosty says.

"I was shocked," Vicki says. "We hadn't talked about marriage. I found out later he and his two roommates and pharmacy classmates, Bill Pigeon and Ken Huff, had talked about it. They predicted he would be the last person of the three to get engaged. He was first."

"Luckily, she said yes," Frosty says. "I loved her and knew she was the one, but being more pragmatic, I thought I'd better wrap this up before we graduated and make sure she would be my military dependent, so that if anything happened to me, she would receive my military benefits."

Frosty and Vicki were married May 18, 1968, in North Bend, her hometown, a month before their graduation from Oregon State. Frosty was 24, Vicki 21.

"We wanted to get married before we graduated, because all of our friends were going to all four corners of the earth," Frosty says.

They had a two-day honeymoon at the Village Green in Cottage Grove. They then drove to Corvallis, where Vicki took her finals and Frosty took his Oregon written pharmacy board exams.

For about nine months, the Comers made their home in Lebanon. Vicki was teaching and Frosty was doing his pharmacy internship at Cent-Wise Drugs there.

"I worked retail on weekends, Christmas and spring breaks, and I got paid $1.25 an hour," Frosty says. "I needed 1,500 total hours to get my Oregon pharmacy license. I had barely 250 when I graduated. I could not go on active duty in the Army until I completed my internship and then pass the practical portion of the pharmacy licensing exam for Oregon."

On April 1, 1969, the Army beckoned. The Comers were about to go on an adventure.

FROSTY'S NO SNOWMAN

Frosty & Vicki in the Army now

CHAPTER 4

Goodbye Cruel World, Hello Army

By January 1969, Frosty Comer had enough intern hours to qualify for his Oregon pharmacist license, but it took a couple of months after he submitted his paperwork for the U.S. Army to schedule him for the 12-week Basic Officers School and one week of Pharmacy Officer School at Fort Sam Houston in San Antonio.

The Comers splurged on a 1968 Dodge Charger, and Vicki's parents gave her father's Pinto to her. Vicki stayed through June 1969 to finish her full-time teaching job in PE and health at Lebanon High. To report on April 1 (what a day to start a military career -- April Fools' Day!) as a First Lieutenant, Frosty drove the Charger to San Antonio to begin 13 weeks of training.

"I also had one week of a pharmacy officer course to gain a pharmacy position in a military medical treatment facility," Frosty says.

Trainees were pretty much 24/7 on the Fort Sam Houston base for those 13 weeks, going through physical training, weapons qualification and military tactics. Vicki flew down one weekend in May to celebrate the Comers' first wedding anniversary. Once training was completed, Frosty returned home to Oregon to await assignment.

"One of the options was to be a helicopter pilot — a dust-off pilot used for emergency patient evacuation from combat zones," he says. "I thought that would be really cool, but I had hay fever, so I didn't qualify."

Many of the American troops were headed for Vietnam as the war heightened.

"Frosty would have been willing to go to Vietnam," Vicki says. "He was very patriotic. But they didn't have pharmacy officers going there."

Frosty had only a two-year commitment, but the Army offered this deal: Sign up for an extra year, you'll be sent to Europe and your wife can go with you.

"We decided to go for it," Frosty says. "We thought we would be sent to Germany."

It would turn out to be Vicenza, Italy, where Frosty would serve as a junior officer in a hospital in Caserma (Camp) Ederle.

In July 1969, the Comers flew from Portland back to San Antonio to pick up their car and drive to Bayonne, N.J., to ship their car to Vicenza, and then to Rome from JFK in New York City. From there, they took a four-hour train ride to Vicenza. It would be their home for the next three years.

"It was a phenomenal time for us," Vicki says, adding with a laugh, "I was pregnant for 18 months of it."

The Comers lived in temporary base housing for a month.

"We had no TV," Frosty says. "We bought a Nordmende AM/FM shortwave radio. We listened to Armed Forces Radio Europe. At nighttime, we would play cards or go to a movie or listen to radio shows. Monday through Friday, I would get up, go across the street to the hospital and start working."

Soon the Comers moved into a two-story, fourplex unit for company grade officers.

"There was a very large play area between the fourplexes," Frosty says. "We would have badminton, croquet and flag football games on the weekends, with a very large demijohn of fresh Italian wine at the ready."

Vicenza was the Southern European Command Headquarters, a region that included Italy, Spain, Greece and Turkey. Frosty, as Chief of Pharmacy, Italy, was responsible for pharmacy operations in the Army hospitals north of Rome, which included a 50-bed hospital in Vicenza and a 25-bed hospital in Livorno. He would need to travel 300 miles to Livorno four to six times a year either by car or helicopter.

Vicki quickly became employed, too, gaining a job for the 1969-70 academic year teaching PE and health and advising the rally squad at the American high school on the Vicenza base.

"Teaching there was really fun," Vicki says. "It wasn't Captain Comer and his wife; it was Mrs. Comer and her husband. I outranked him. I taught the kids of the generals and colonels. They knew me, but not Frosty, until they came to the hospital. I was in charge of the cheerleaders."

One of the more memorable high school basketball games was in Trento, Italy. Vicki took the cheer team and Frosty was able to attend. After the game, the basketball team, coaches and cheer team were bused back to Vicenza but the Trento school administrators wanted to treat the Vicenza teachers to an eight-course course dinner and a visit to one of the castles that had been turned into a wine-making school.

"Vicki and I had driven to Trento, and I had to get back for a 7 a.m. troop sick call and a 9 a.m. dependent sick call," Frosty says. "However, we were told we needed to stay. After the dinner we visited the 'wine castle' and drank and laughed and giggled and sang with the Italians, who loved the Americans for liberating them from the Nazis. That was still fresh in their minds."

The four-hour drive back to Vicenza through the Italian Alps was challenging.

"We got back around 6 a.m., in time for me to shower, change and make the 7 a.m. sick call," Frosty says. "I would say Vicki and I improved international relationships with the Trento Italian school district that time."

The Comers didn't wait long for parenthood to happen. Frosty attended a two-week nuclear biological and chemical weapons warfare school in Germany.

"Soon after I returned to the base in February 1970, Wendy was conceived," he says.

Wendy was born in November 1970. "We knew we wanted another child," Vicki says. "I got pregnant again."

Vicki quit her teaching job after one year. Molly was born in March 1972.

❄

Through his three years in Italy, Frosty was a pharmacy officer with 26 extra duties.

"For instance, I was the Secret Documents Officer for the hospital," he says. "I was responsible for hospital's secret documents for any medical support of troop activities in Italy and on the Mediterranean. I filled in as the assistant adjutant, assist supply officer, assistant registrar, linen officer, nuclear incident/accident officer, administrative officer of the day and weekends and the executive officer of the hospital at times. I also had to account for every capital piece of equipment, and sometimes expendable items as the property book officer."

How did he like all the extra stuff?

"I hated it," he says. "You are property of the Army. Your specialty is medicine or pharmacy, but you are a soldier first. I wanted to be a pharmacy officer, but I had all these extra duties. I had to do them, and while I did them, I learned how to run a hospital."

So there was a silver lining.

"It was a forced education that I didn't truly appreciate until later, when I got into more senior positions and came to understand how you have to work together," Frosty says. "There is a slogan in the Army, 'You can't run a hospital without linen.' In other words, one department cannot run a hospital. You need every department working in unison.

"You get so focused on your profession, you think you are the center of the universe. You ain't. Nobody is. Even the doctors aren't. You must treat everybody as a customer."

At Vicenza, Army forces had tactical nuclear weapons to defend the Fulda Gap that would stop the USSR tanks from breaking through to the French coast in 3 days. Frosty was tasked as the executive officer of the medical unit that would support the Army with refreshing the nuclear warheads.

"If one fell off a truck, it wouldn't explode, but you could have nuclear materials spread over the ground," he says. "You had to have security, medical and signal (communications). Luckily, I never had to deploy to do that, but we had to train for it.

"I had to work hard to have a good attitude about doing all the extra duties, but once I learned them, I was able to start doing some of the pharmacy stuff I'd been reading about. I became a much more complete pharmacy and military officer."

During the times Frosty was on leave, "we saw a lot of the country, and we enjoyed it," Vicki says. "Over the three years we were stationed in Vicenza, we went to Germany, Belgium, France, Spain, Austria,

Switzerland, England and Scotland. We traveled all over. Frosty's mother and aunt came over, and my mother came over after Wendy was born."

Frosty, who was anxious to learn what was going on in the U.S. with hospital pharmacy, became a member of the American Society of Hospital Pharmacists. In the ASHP monthly journal, Frosty read an article about hospitals starting a unit dose and IV admixture medication system and the practice of preparing daily doses for hospitalized patients.

"Nurses at our 45th Field Hospital wouldn't let me do that, and the chief nurse outranked me," Frosty says. "So I wrote a proposal that went to the commander."

The commander was Colonel Henry Mendez, who later became a 3-star Lieutenant General and Surgeon General of the U.S. Army. Frosty's proposal was accepted with the support of Dr. Heyward Harry Nettles, who was the Comers' next-door neighbor and pediatrician who helped deliver both Comers' daughters."

Dr. Nettles' 3-year-old son, Heyward Junior, had contracted the flu, was extremely dehydrated and was admitted to the 45 Field Hospital.

"Luckily, I visited him shortly after his admission," Frosty says. "I discovered the nurse had started a 3 percent saline IV on instead of a Dextrose 5 percent and one-third normal saline IV -- nine times the salt that was ordered. Had the one liter of 3 percent saline been completely administered, it could have killed him. Needless to say, all the nursing, medical and pharmacy staff were very upset."

Staff members were supportive of Frosty in starting his new unit dose and IV admixture program the following week. This "double check" between the nurse and pharmacist is now the standard of practice in all American hospitals.

"The big advantage of these centralized systems is that the nurse is relieved of much of her pharmaceutical work load and is free to concentrate on nursing duties," Frosty was quoted as saying in a 1971 article of Stars & Stripes, the daily American European military newspaper.

Frosty was beginning to catch the attention of his superiors. In summer of 1971, the pharmacy consultant to the Army surgeon general rode with him in his car on the troop train from Frankfurt to West Berlin. They were to attend a conference where Frosty was to present his unit dose and IV admixture program to the European Military Pharmacy Conference. The pharmacy consultant wanted Frosty to commit to the Voluntary Indefinite Army status that would mean an Army Pharmacy career.

"They were going to send me to grad school and do a residency at Walter Reed, Madigan or one of the other big Army hospitals," he says. "I would become a career pharmacy officer and perhaps one day be the pharmacy consultant to the Army surgeon general."

After consulting with Vicki about this big decision, Frosty committed to the required Voluntary Indefinite status. But he thought his next stop would be Corvallis. In the fall of 1971, he applied for enrollment in the Masters program in the OSU College of Pharmacy for hospital pharmacy administration and was accepted for the fall of '72.

"We were in Vicenza, preparing to find an apartment in Corvallis," Frosty says. "The Army was going to pay me as a Captain. They were going to pay my tuition, books and housing at Oregon State. My job was to get a Masters degree. But then the residence program for active-duty pharmacy officers was suspended indefinitely. Frosty's orders were changed due to the drawdown of troops and programs at the end of the Viet Nam war.

"All of a sudden, in early 1972, I got orders to report to Madigan

Army Medical Center (MAMC) at Fort Lewis," Frosty says. "I had signed up for 'voluntary indefinite.' I owed them another year at least. I had to go."

In the summer of '72, now with two young daughters, Frosty arrived at Madigan to become the assistant chief of pharmacy.

"I was being sent to a 1,000-bed hospital," he says. "That was an incredible jump. I was pissed off because I wasn't going to school. Because I was so disappointed, I put in my papers to get out of the military, reapplied to OSU College of Pharmacy and was accepted again. But I still needed to complete one more year of my military Voluntary Indefinite commitment."

Once military housing was assigned, the Comers set up house at Fort Lewis, Wash. They were there from June 1972 to August 1973.

"It turned out to be a great assignment," Frosty says. "The MAMC job was a huge jump in my career assignments. I 'jumped' over several other senior captains when I was given this assignment. Going from a 50-bed hospital to a 1,000-bed hospital and filling 3,000 prescriptions a day was very big."

At Madigan, Frosty was a Captain filling a Lieutenant Colonel position. His boss, Linn Danielski, was a Major filling a Colonel position. Both were performing jobs two ranks above what they were supposed to be.

"We were young and weren't afraid of making significant improvements," Frosty says. "We implemented a lot of automation in the outpatient pharmacies that decreased prescription filling times and started providing IV sterile solutions to the inpatients. This was all done with only three pharmacy officers and about a dozen pharmacy technicians."

Vicki was for now a full-time mother. Frosty was moonlighting at a Tacoma retail pharmacy three nights a week to make some extra money.

At the time, Madigan was one of the major medical centers for the military that was receiving a lot of wounded soldiers from Vietnam while also taking care of local troops, dependents and retirees.

Says Frosty: "MAMC gave me an incredible experience in managing large volume work in a very complex healthcare environment that served me well for graduate school and my career."

❄

Frosty enjoyed his time at MAMC and working with Linn and was having second thoughts about leaving the Army, but decided graduate school was his best option. He submitted papers to be discharged and transferred to the Active Army Reserve medical unit in Vancouver, Wash., in September 1973.

The Comers moved to Corvallis and lived in adult student housing for a year. At the age of 29, Frosty started his Masters program in hospital pharmacy administration at Oregon State with a wife, two young daughters and very little money in reserve.

"In Oregon, if you wanted to get a career as hospital pharmacy administrator, you needed to get a Masters degree and do a residency," he says. "I had been told if I didn't get a 3-point GPA in grad school, I was going to get kicked out. What I found, as I was going to classes with 20- and 21-year-olds, was how much I had learned from being in the military that was never taught in school. Despite taking several difficult courses, I was a much better student. I had to get serious since my family's future was at stake."

Frosty was a teaching assistant (TA) to his previous professor, Harriet Sisson. The classes he taught at the College of Pharmacy for the 1973-74 academic year included six labs of two hours each Monday through Friday.

"If I had failed my academic classes and not done a good job as a TA, I would probably have been kicked out of grad school and worked in one of my grandfather's drug stores, which wouldn't have been the end of the world," he says. "Many hospitals had residency programs. I wanted to get a Masters and residency so I could punch those tickets and be a good candidate for any director of pharmacy position. I was ahead of my time. The military had introduced this concept to me."

To help with finances, he transferred to the Active Army Reserves, where he made $150 a month. Frosty used that and funds from the GI bill and his teaching assistant salary to pay for grad school and housing.

"I was a teaching assistant for compounding and dispensing," he says. "Harriet was great, but she didn't have a lab manual for the class. I ended up writing the lab manual for each of the three quarters."

Sisson reviewed and approved it. It was published and was put into the OSU Bookstore for students to use when they took the class.

"I put together my grad program, which included an industrial engineering class that was basically work-flow analysis," Frosty says. "Also, I had a personnel management class from the College of Business and several grad-level pharmacy classes."

Frosty also did rounds at Oregon Health Sciences University in Portland.

"I would spend a couple of nights a month on the psychiatric unit and surgery, watching how a civilian hospital operated," he says. "I had been in an Army hospital pharmacy for 4 1/2 years and had to learn how the civilian hospitals worked. The hospital systems made money and administrators controlled the purse strings. It was a different environment."

If Frosty wasn't busy enough, he also joined the Army Reserve unit in Vancouver, Wash., serving as chief of pharmacy for the 313th Convalescence Center, which eventually became the 313th MASH unit.

"That paid a critical $150 a month for our family," Frosty says. "I would go once a month for a weekend drill. It was not an active hospital. It was an Army Reserve unit that trained on weekends and during the two-week annual training, usually in the summer."

Frosty made quick friends at Fort Vancouver with Dennis Rogers and Cabot Clark. All three studied pharmacy at Oregon State. "Three musky steers," Clark cracks.

"We met in the 313th MASH unit," Rogers says. "I was a Sergeant at the time and Frosty was a Captain. I was in pharmacy school and he was in pharmacy graduate school. I got my commission after I graduated. I wasn't acting as a pharmacy officer. I was a supply officer once I got my commission.

"Frosty joined the unit and introduced himself. He wondered, why is this pharmacy student working in supply? He had to tell me about this New England Journal of Medicine case study about this jogger who went running on a real cold day and had penile frostbite. That's Frosty."

"We connected really well during that time," says Frosty, who has a story to tell on Rogers, too.

After both had graduated, Frosty from graduate school with his Masters and Dennis from pharmacy school, they deployed for their annual two-week training sessions as military pharmacists.

"One year Dennis went to Peru and staffed a mobile Army surgical hospital to provide care for a rural community," Frosty says. "It was really good training to be able to know how to thrive in chaos."

Then there was the year Dennis and Frosty went to Silas B. Hayes Army Hospital at Fort Ord in Monterey, Calif. There were two top military golf courses on the base. Frosty, an excellent linksman, brought his clubs with him. Rogers, who didn't play golf, acted as caddy for a round, pulling the golf cart.

"Just above the course on a bluff was all the generals' housing," Frosty says. "We were on a par-3 and the tee box was right below their houses. I wanted Dennis to be on his best behavior. I hit a great shot — almost a hole in one — and headed to the green. I asked for my putter, and before you know it, Dennis was pulling the golf cart halfway across the green."

Frosty liked Dennis — "he was a sweetheart of a guy" — and they have remained friends since. In 1988, Frosty set him up with his wife, Lou Anne, who worked with Frosty at Good Samaritan Hospital.

"We went out to dinner together," Rogers says. "Lou Anne was worried about meeting me because I lived in Madras at the time. She was afraid I would be wearing jeans and cowboy boots. We got married in 1990."

Through the '80s, Frosty and Dennis both attended three years of officers advance courses, then three years at the U.S. Army Command and General Staff School in Vancouver.

"One night a week from October through May, with an extra two-week annual training," Frosty says.

There were two military hospitals in Vancouver at the time. The other was the 45th Station Hospital, where Cabot Clark was stationed. Frosty, Dennis and Cab would all be deployed together in 1990 for the first Desert Shield/Desert Storm.

Cab Clark is a South Salem High graduate.

"I tended bar and raised a little hell around Salem after I graduated," Clark says. "In 1961, three buddies and I joined the Air Force in the buddy program. I spent six years in the Air Force as a pharmacy technician, mostly in France. I came back to Oregon and got accepted to the school of pharmacy at Oregon State. I finished it up two years after Frosty did. I didn't really know him at Oregon State. I had heard the name, but he was an upperclassman."

Clark tried to return to the Air Force as a commissioned pharmacy officer, "but at the time, they were taking graduate pharmacists and directly assigning them as enlisted men. I said, 'Nah, I'm not even an enlisted man. Not interested.'"

Clark married and started raising a family and was working at a Fred Meyer pharmacy in Eugene, Ore. One day, he got a call from a physician who was the commander of the 45th Station Hospital at Fort Vancouver. He was looking for a pharmacist.

"Six months later, I got a letter from the president of the United States, welcoming me to the Army Reserve," Clark says. "That started my career at Fort Vancouver.

"Frosty is a sweetheart. One of the most fun guys I have ever had the pleasure of associating with. He has a good spirit, a good portion of devil still under his skin. We hit it off as far as hell-raising with our reserve time at Fort Vancouver. We probably had a reputation that irritated the hell out of the nursing crew. There was always something going on."

A decade later, they reconnected at Desert Storm. But that is getting well ahead of the story.

FROSTY'S NO SNOWMAN

Marshfield High School, Coos Bay, Oregon

Bay Area Hospital, Coos Bay, Oregon

CHAPTER 5

CHANGING THE DRUGS PARADIGM

After one year attending classes for his Masters degree at Oregon State in June 1974, Frosty Comer moved with his family to take part in the American Society of Hospital Pharmacists residency program in Coos Bay.

A new facility, the Bay Area Hospital, had just been built. Administrators Richard Graybeal and Jon Mitchel hired a director of pharmacy, Ron Coberly, who had completed his Masters and residency in North Carolina and had gotten approval to start the first ASHP residency in Oregon at the hospital in June 1974.

"It couldn't have happened at a better time," Frosty says. "God was smiling on us."

Unfortunately, tragedy struck. In May 1974, a month before the Comers were to move to the Coos Bay/North Bend area, Vicki's father, Curly Leininger, died of a heart attack. He was 52.

"Curly was an icon in Coos and Curry Counties," Frosty says. "Everybody loved him. Such a great guy. He had become a surrogate father to me. It was so sad. After we moved down there in June, we helped Vicki's mom deal with the death of her husband."

Says Vicki: "Dad treated Frosty like a son, and Frosty treated him like his father."

The weekend before Curly passed, he and wife Connie had joined Frosty, Vicki and their two young daughters at a motel in Florence.

"We went out to dinner and danced with my folks," Vicki recalls. "Then Frosty took the girls back to the room, and I spent some time with Mom and Dad by myself. I got to spend some special time with Dad, not knowing that was going to be the last time."

While Frosty was doing his residency, Vicki was serving as a PE and health teacher and tennis coach at Marshfield High in Coos Bay.

"My mom was by herself after Dad died," Vicki says. "We spent a lot of time with her. The girls were at a babysitter quite a bit."

As part of his Masters program at OSU during the 1973-74 school year, Frosty wrote a thesis entitled

"Comparison of Shared and Traditional Pharmacy Services in Small Hospitals.

"I pulled from my experience working in Italy," Frosty says. "The thesis can be found in the library at Oregon State today."

Bay Area Hospital was a 140-bed facility that replaced two smaller hospitals, which had previously been in Coos Bay and North Bend. There were smaller hospitals in the southern Oregon coast communities of Reedsport (25 beds), Coquille (20), Gold Beach (15) and Bandon (5). BAH was the primary referral hospital in Coos and Curry counties when a higher level of care was needed. Never a shrinking violet, Frosty convinced BAH administrators to let him pick a hospital to do a trial. It turned out to be Gold Beach. Frosty's first task was to take inventory of their medication room and found that 25 percent of their drugs were overstocked or out of date.

"While taking the inventory, I observed an employee who walked into the drug room and, in front of me, took a couple of Tylenol No. 3 that had 30 mg of codeine and went back to work in the business office of the hospital," he says. "It was an example of a total lack of drug control."

Frosty sought out a hospital administrator and told him what had happened. He also found a 500-tablet bottle of Quaaludes. Only two tablets had been used from it and the drugs had expired.

"I asked the head nurse, who was responsible for drug purchasing, why she had purchased such a large bottle when there were much smaller sizes available," Frosty says. "She said, 'The drug salesman told me if I'd buy a bottle of 500, it would be cheaper by the tablet.' My thought was, not when you have to throw out 498 tablets because they expired." Frosty helped enact a procedural change in which the hospital converted to a "unit-dose" system.

"We would send them unit doses of the drugs they needed in quantities of 10 or 20s so they wouldn't expire," he says. "That's called supply discipline."

Frosty learned to finesse suggested changes.

"You can't always be a bull in a china closet," he says. "There is more than one way to fix things. You must develop consensus-building skills when you are playing in someone else's sandbox."

Frosty's time with the military in Italy had planted firm beliefs.

"By the time I was at BAH, I had fallen in love with the collaborative interdisciplinary environment of the military health system," he says. "A pharmacist is a partner with doctors and nurses in health care. That appealed to me. We were doing more than just providing pills. We were giving the right drug to the right patient at the right time with the right information. That was our focus in the military.

"When I was doing my internship at Cent-Wise (in the late '60s), if the doctor wrote a prescription and the patient asked me, 'What is this for and how am I supposed to take it?,' I couldn't tell them and had to refer them back to their doctor to answer their questions."

Students were required to pass a typing test to graduate from pharmacy school.

"I couldn't have a technician type of label," Frosty says. "Because of Oregon's pharmacy laws, I had to type it. This was a definite change from my Army pharmacy experience."

An Army pharmacy technician taught Comer how to compound sterile products, which wasn't covered in pharmacy school.

"Things were so unprofessional in the '60s," he says. "Drug information knowledge was not used. You were a highly educated, highly paid vending machine.

"My generation created the collaborative interdisciplinary environment and the operational systems that provided necessary drug control and safety. When I was in the Army in Italy, it was a smaller facility, and a much more collaborative interdisciplinary and family atmosphere."

After a year, Vicki chose to put her work on hold.

"I loved teaching and coaching, but we had the girls," she says. "I told Frosty, 'We planned both of our daughters, and we are not spending the time we need to with them,' and he totally agreed. I didn't go to work again until they both were in grade school. I would always be home when the kids got back from school."

❄

Frosty had finished his thesis work at BAH but hadn't written it yet when he was hired as staff pharmacist at Good Samaritan Hospital in Portland in 1975.

"I was hired for a position I was technically overqualified for," Frosty says.

Good Sam was a 539-bed tertiary care hospital, not a primary care hospital but a critical care hospital for specialty services such as cardiac, neurology and oncology. It was the biggest hospital at the time in Oregon, though not as big as Madigan.

Jim Sanger was Good Sam's director of pharmacy and the man who hired Frosty.

"One of those decisions I've always regretted," Sanger jokes.

Sanger is a native of Bird Island, Minn., and an educated man. He holds a degree in pharmacy from Creighton, a Master's degree from Purdue and a Masters of Business Administration from Adelphi. Jim had also been a Lieutenant in the Navy.

"Frosty was like I was," Sanger says. "He had a military background. He had done a residency at Bay Area Hospital in Coos Bay. I was looking for somebody with leadership skills and a little advanced training. Frosty was perfect for what we needed.

"When I got hired at Good Sam, the pharmacy department was significantly behind with contemporary services. It was pretty much an old drugstore concept. Orders came down, pharmacists filled them and not a lot else was going on. We needed to upgrade the services dramatically."

During their six years working together, Sanger and Comer, along with other pharmacists, implemented several unique hospital pharmacy services, including home IV therapy, a unit-dose system, IV admixtures and an ICU pharmacy satellite system.

"Jim wanted to do it," Frosty says, "and I was one of a perfect group of pharmacists he hired to do this."

"We started with home IV therapy," Sanger says. "We had a unique situation in that it wasn't just a pharmacy department, it was also an IV therapy department. We had IV therapy nurses as part of the department. They were taking care of the IV duties for the hospital. We combined them, and when Frosty got there, we implemented a whole new way of handling IV therapy. We got pharmacy techs working on preparation and nurses would start the lines and get the first fluids going.

"Unique to the times, we had a labeling system that allowed the labels on the IV bags to have multiple copies. You could pull off a label and affix it to the patient's chart. It eliminated the handwriting and transcribing that had been necessary before. The nurse could send down a copy and say, 'Waiting for orders,' or 'Please fill.' That combination of things simplified the whole process."

Frosty loved the change he was able to bring about at Good Sam. It meant breaking down some figurative barriers with nurses.

"We were becoming a one-stop shop for medicines and IV, but we still had a lot of convincing to do with the nurses," Frosty says. "Jim got the support of hospital administrators, but when you are trying to change the way nurses were doing things, and they had done it for decades, it's hard.

"We tried to sell it as, 'We are here to make your job easier (to nurses and doctors).' We centralized all the pharmaceutical inventory along with the IV supplies and tubing, and the IV pumps. That put a lot of pressure on the pharmacy department to perform. The nurses were used to going into their mini pharmacy to get what they wanted when they wanted it."

During that time, Good Sam began using hyperalimentation (total parenteral nutrition).

"When, for whatever reason, a patient couldn't take sufficient nutrition by mouth to stay alive, food would be delivered through IV therapy," Sanger says. "Paulette Egging wrote the first manual for the delivery, and Frosty had a huge role in that whole thing. When Frosty left Good Sam, he and Paulette started their own Home IV Therapy company and used a lot of the things they had learned at Good Sam in their new enterprise."

Comer and Sanger became golfing companions and good friends.

"Frosty is an Energizer Bunny type," Jim says. "Constantly on the go. He is a driven guy. He wants to get stuff done. He is extremely positive, hard-working, innovative, a very good-hearted guy. Frosty is just a really good person to be with."

In the years when their legs were spry, the two played pick-up basketball together.

"Frosty was the guard and I was the shooting forward," Sanger says. "We had these routines we would use where we would set a pick-and-roll, I would roll to the basket and either he would get a jumper or I would get a layup. We worked pretty darn well together on the basketball court."

Frosty had another friend who was a hospital pharmacy director. Rick Sahli worked at Providence. Sahli liked hoops, too, so they scheduled a game between staff members of the pharmacies at the two hospitals.

"We had a full court at a local church, and we got some of the ladies on staff to come and be cheerleaders," Sahli says. "They absolutely blitzed us. Frosty was a really quick little point guard and his boss, Jim Sanger, he could shoot the lights out."

Sahli sought payback. A few months later, the teams scheduled a rematch.

"I had hired this kid to work in our stock room," Rick says. "He was about 6-10 and coordinated. He dominated and we got even.

Frosty and I have been going after each other on the ball courts and golf courses ever since."

Sahli grew up in the San Francisco Bay Area and graduated from pharmacy at Oregon State in 1971. Soon thereafter he was hired as director of pharmacy for the Providence Health System.

"During the late '70s, hospital pharmacy was a small pond, so to speak," Sahli says. "It was a relatively new profession. Most hospitals didn't have pharmacies until the '60s. Frosty and I were fortunate enough to work in hospital pharmacy during a period of a lot of growth and change. We went from small departments with very few employees to where we were big and important, with a lot of employees. It became a 24-hour, seven-days-a-week operation. We were a close-knit group of people with a common interest working in hospitals. We were members of the Oregon Society of Hospital Pharmacists.

"Frosty and I had meetings once a month, a chance to get to know others and swap stories. Somewhere along the line, we discovered we both liked to play golf. We have been doing that with each other ever since. Frosty is a very competitive person. He loves to compete whether it is sports, business or whatever. I am a bit of a competitor myself, so we had that in common."

The Oregon Society of Hospital Pharmacists is the association of pharmacists who work in the state. "Because of all the ancillary services we developed, entities like Legacy, Providence and Keizer are called health systems, where they have insurance and provider capabilities," Comer says. "We learned from each other and became more of a legislative force to improve the pharmaceutical care in hospitals and health systems."

Through the years Sahli and Comer worked in collaboration with each other, there were many changes in the business.

"One of the things a lot of hospital pharmacies were trying to do was get more involved in clinical services — instead of dispensing drugs and IV solutions, we wanted to be more involved in actual decision-making with patient drug therapy," Sahli says. "It was difficult to convince leadership positions to give us the time and manpower to get more involved. But we were really pushing that, and we all shared stuff with each other. You can't do that nowadays. But in those days, there was a lot or sharing of information and ideas.

"We got pharmacists up on the nursing stations, and they basically sold their talents to the nurses and physicians and got used more. We were trying to create more opportunities for that. There was a change in how our physicians and pharmacists were being educated. The older physicians were very independent practitioners, captains of the ship. They called all the shots; everybody did what they wanted. They were fiercely independent, skeptical and critical of anyone trying to tell them how to practice medicine."

That began to change in the '80s.

"In many medical training programs, the physicians were in classes with pharmacists, and there was a shift to a more collaborative practice — a team taking care of the patients," Sahli says. "They were getting educated to this thing. That helped us, so younger guys and gals coming in were more in tune to that coming into the profession."

One of Sahli's missions was to establish a clinic practice for pharmacists.

"We went on a little fundraising program," he says. "We wrote grant applications to some pharmaceutical companies and did other things to raise money. The goal was, if we could raise enough money to hire a pharmacist, we would turn him or her loose for a two-year job and say, 'Now make yourself indispensable.'"

Sahli asked a number of doctors how they would use a pharmacist in their office.

"Some said, 'Why would I need that?' " he says. "Others said, 'I would have them help manage my difficult patients or help manage refills.' We collected information and planted a seed, raised enough money and went to the administration, and they said we could hire a pharmacist at Providence."

It worked so well that, by the time Sahli left Providence in 2009, it was a totally different picture for hospital pharmacists.

"The pharmacy group had spun off into the different branches of the hospital system," Sahli says. "There must have been 20 to 30 employees — half of them pharmacists and half of them pharmacy technicians running the refill programs for hundreds of physicians. A sea change from 25 years earlier."

❄

The Oregon Society of Hospital Pharmacists worked with the state's retail pharmacy associations, Oregon State Pharmacists Association, to get the legislature to pass legislation that allowed the State Board of Pharmacy to promulgate rules and regulations for the use of pharmacy technicians, which freed up pharmacists for more of a clinical and educational role.

Among the other legislative successes for the OSHP: Development of drug formularies, expansion of hospital services in the home and community, group purchasing and overall improvement and cost effectiveness of pharmaceutical care in hospital and health systems.

"At Good Samaritan Hospital in the mid '70s, we developed the first hospital formulary so we could lower our drug costs through bidding for generically equivalent drugs from different manufacturers," Frosty says. "There was a huge physician and drug manufacturers pushback. Hospital and health care costs were rising fast, and this was our opportunity to use competitive bidding to reduce the cost of generic drugs. The next step was developing a formulary that included therapeutic equivalent drugs. We had a pharmacy and therapeutics committee, comprised of doctors coming from different specialties. They were in charge of working with us on the drugs they used for their practices."

One of the issues the OSHP tackled with the Oregon legislature was getting approval for generic substitution.

"For example, there are multiple kinds of hay fever medicines with equivalent chemical structures, but they all help," Frosty says. "They are all either generically or therapeutically equivalent. When we bid equivalent drugs with manufacturers, our cost of drugs relative to what they had been before were significantly lowered.

"Jim worked with specific physician specialties to create a list of drugs to include in our hospital formulary that could be substituted (for brand-name drugs), unless a physician specifically wrote to not substitute. We became collegial partners with physicians providing better cost-effective pharmaceutical care to patients.

Good Sam became Oregon's first civilian hospital to do this that was not an HMO provider organization."

The employees at Good Samaritan had the green light to be progressive.

"Jim was the one who said, 'Let's ask for forgiveness and get resources later,' " Frosty says. "We were Nike before Nike, with the 'Just Do It' motto. We were allowed to try new things, make mistakes and correct quickly.

"We were able to create one of the most progressive pharmacy practices in the country. We had pharmacists on the nursing stations who were working with the doctors and nurses when the prescription was first written to make sure it was correct and they had the right information. We had a very active ICU satellite pharmacy with our pharmacists on the code team. And we were beginning to manage chronic disease patients."

❄

Though he was very involved in work and business and was a husband and father of two young girls, Frosty found time for a recreational endeavor. The Comers had moved to a home in Beaverton across the street from Jay and Linda Johnson. Jay was a member of the Mount Hood Ski Patrol. During the Comers' time in Italy, they had taken "some amazing trips in the Alps." In 1975, Frosty applied to volunteer with the Mount Hood Ski Patrol, "but I flunked the hill test." For the next year, he served in the first-aid rooms of Timberline, Meadows and Ski Bowl/Multorpor ski areas and honed his skiing.

"One day, Jay — who was the head of the training program — was skiing behind me," Frosty says. "He remarked how bow-legged I was. He took me into a ski shop and put me on a boot canting machine, which made my skis flat."

The next year, Frosty passed the hill test. He wound up as a member of the MHSP hill patrol for nine years.

"My young daughters were becoming very good skiers, so the last year on the patrol I was an apprentice trainer," he says. "Working with new patrollers was a blast; I really enjoyed that. I wasn't the best skier, but because of my medical background, if someone got injured, I was useful."

CHAPTER 6

Death with Dignity

In 1979, Frosty Comer was promoted to assistant director of pharmacy at Good Samaritan Hospital and Medical Center. From 1985-89, he served as the hospital's associate director of pharmacy. By that time, many of the changes he had helped initiated in hospital pharmacy were well-established. There were, however, always challenges.

"Once we got the unit dose and sterile product preparation systems up and running, Dr. Dick Drake came to the pharmacy one day and said many of his patients had gotten horrible cases of peritonitis in the intensive care unit," Frosty says. "He asked me to check into it. I went to the ICU. Nurses were preparing peritoneal dialysis solution in a dirty linen room next to a sink. Once we got Dr. Drake's support and prepared this important sterile product in our inpatient pharmacy IV Laminar flow hoods, the infections stopped cold."

Hospital pharmacy officials expanded the types of critical care IV sterile product from the inpatient pharmacy. Because the inpatient pharmacy was in the basement of the hospital and the ICU was on the second floor, Frosty consulted with the head ICU nurse, Amy Labinski.

She agreed to give up her office in the ICU, and it was turned into a small satellite pharmacy that could also compound critical sterile

IV solutions when immediately needed. It became the first pharmacy satellite for ICUs staffed by pharmacists in the state of Oregon.

As a result of that, Good Sam pharmacists were included in the "cardiac code" team.

"We all had to go through advanced cardiac training," Frosty says. "Our primary function was to quickly do the dosing calculations and prepare all the medications or IVs that would be used during a cardiac arrest wherever it was in the hospital."

At the time, there were no inpatient hospice facilities in the U.S.

In 1979, Frosty was appointed as advisor to the hospice program for the Visiting Nurses Association of Portland, whose director was Linda Van Buren.

The timing was both poignant and heartbreaking. One of Frosty's twin sisters, Kim, started having blood in her urine. She was diagnosed with kidney cancer. She was 27. Ironically, Kim was a nurse. So was older sister Casey.

"It had an impact on the hospice program in the city of Portland," Frosty says.

Linda Van Buren became the hospice nurse for Kim. Kim's husband, Bob Nichols, was a physician. At the time of Kim's diagnosis, they lived in Chelan, Wash. They moved to Portland so Kim could get the care from her brother and the VNA hospice program.

"We ended up taking care of Kim completely at Mom's house in Hillsdale," Frosty says.

Most of the caretakers' mission was relieving pain and symptoms.

"In those days, we did not have patient-controlled analgesic pumps, that are now the size of a big iPhone," Frosty says. "They are used to provide a basal (steady) rate of IV infusion of morphine with a bolus dose, usually every 15 minutes, if needed," Frosty explains. "We had central catheters that were inserted into the chest wall.

"The reason you need to access this larger vein is you can't inject some medications in a peripheral vein that are too concentrated for a small blood vessel."

In addition, peripheral IV sites have to be changed frequently, and Kim had a central catheter.

"We were able to administer IV morphine, only via IV push on a schedule that was based on her pain needs, Total Parenteral Nutrition, anti-nausea medication and hydration," Frosty says. "The tumor started blocking off her stomach. At that point, she was still a viable human being. We didn't want her to die of starvation. She couldn't eat orally or keep her nutrition up."

For about three months, Frosty provided daily total parenteral nutrition in the central IV catheter, that she could infuse over an eight-hour period.

"For pain and symptom control, Casey and I, and sometimes Bob, would administer prescriptions for IV morphine, Seconal (barbiturate), hydration, and anti-nausea drugs that were ordered by her oncologist, Dr. Al Brady," Frosty says. "I would prepare them at our Good Sam pharmacy for Kim. "Typically, these were patients who were put in a nursing home or the hospital and frequently died without having their pain and symptoms properly treated. But we were far more medically prepared than your typical hospice family. We were able to prove this could be done at the home and it could be taught to those who didn't have the expertise we did."

Through the 1970s and early 1980s, home infusion therapy wasn't the standard practice.

"It was an industry that got started when the IV pumps, catheters such as the PICC (peripherally inserted central catheter) and central lines were invented," Frosty says. "This new technology allowed us to do things at home that used to be only done in the hospital. This is the genesis of modern-day pharmacy and nursing care in the home. I was fortunate enough to be on the front lines of the development of hospital care in the home — acute care utilizing therapies that used to only be done in the hospital."

Kim's last months were exacting on her, the family and brother. Frosty feels fortunate he had great help.

"I had to go into a very clinical state of mind to control myself and the situation," he says. "Dr. Brady was an amazing person, and so was Linda Van Buren. They made a very difficult situation better."

As Kim's cancer progressed, Dr. Brady taught Frosty how to manage pain via morphine for cancer patients "without zonking them out," Frosty says.

"Since we didn't have the new PCA pumps available, we had to administer Kim's pain and nausea meds via IV push on a schedule that was dictated by her pain and symptoms both day and night," Frosty says. "A few years later, with the invention of the PCA pumps, you could program the pump to provide a much lower continuous dose of morphine, via IV or subcutaneously, and program the pump to administer a bolus does every 15 minutes, if needed for breakthrough pain or a patient's activity that caused additional pain."

Kim's tumor enlarged, and it became more difficult to manage the symptoms. The hospice nurse caring for her inserted a nasal gastric (NG) tube.

"Nursing homes and hospitals were not equipped to handle this kind of patient," Frosty says. "They were dying, and it takes high touch as well as high tech to take care of them. In essence, the hospitals gave up on them, and people got tired of their relatives dying in pain in hospitals. We, as healthcare providers and institutions were not doing a good job taking care of patients at their end of life."

Home infusion therapy played a major role in improving end-of-life care.

"My sister's situation (in the early '80s) helped introduce me to how we can take care of patients at end of life in the home, which now has become standard practice," Frosty says. "It led to me having the clinical confidence to go to doctors around the state and say, 'Refer your cancer patients to me. I'll make sure they get the best pain and symptom management.'

"It wasn't just me. We had pharmacists and administrators at Good Samaritan supporting us with Kim. They were allowing me to provide end-of-life pharmacy care to my sister in my mom's home in Hillsdale."

Frosty stayed strong for his sister as her life slipped away. Kim Nichols passed away on May 19, 1981.

"Afterward, you just lose it," he says. "But then you rally and think, 'What did I learn, and how I can help people in the future and advance the treatment that other people don't get?' The loss of my sister was very difficult, but it created a passion in me."

Kim's story, and those of others, led to the passing of Oregon ballot Measure 16, the "Death With Dignity" act. Measure 16, which legalized medical aid in dying, passed in 1994. It was the nation's first law to give terminally ill adults the option to obtain a physician's prescription for ending one's life.

"In the years before that, if the health care system couldn't cure you, they typically abandoned you," Comer says. "Too many patients died without the needed pain and symptom management therapies. The only saving grace was hospice."

Portland VNA was the only real hospice program in Portland at the time. Frosty's background, and the inspiration he drew from his departed sister, helped him play a major part in the development of the home IV therapy industry and the development of Portland's "Hospice House."

By 1983, Medicare had changed its hospital reimbursement system from cost-based to a diagnosis-related group (DRG). After the Medicare implementation of the DRG payment system, the hospital was paid a set amount based on the diagnosis.

"Let's say you went in for an appendectomy and the hospital got paid $10,000 if you were there one day or 10 days," Comer says. "At Good Sam, our average length of stay in 1983 was 9 1/2 days. That was typical of hospitals in the state."

By that time, Good Sam already had an effective and functional home IV therapy, hospice, home health and medical supply services programs.

"We were ready to get the people out of the hospital sooner," Frosty says. "By 1985, the average hospital length of stay dropped to five days, almost cut in half. That meant we had to do the same amount of work in almost half the time, but we didn't need as many beds. Every year since the implementation of DRGs, the average has gone down. Today, the average length of stay is under four days in the state of Oregon. You have a lot of out-patient surgeries. It has significantly reduced the cost of health care. The challenge to providers? You still must do the same amount of work in fewer days and still take care of any post-hospital care needs of the patient."

❄

In 1983, Dr. Tom Buell, an English professor at Portland State, went on a one-year sabbatical to London with wife Joan. She was a teacher at Catlin Gabel who volunteered at an England inpatient hospice facility. In the U.S. at the time, hospice programs were all in the home. When Joan returned, she committed to building an in-patient hospice program in Portland, which would come to be called "Hospice House."

"Joan was an amazing leader and patient advocate," Frosty says.

Frosty's mother, Connie, wanted to help after the experience of losing her daughter, Kim.

"I'm not quite sure how Mom and Joan connected, but they did," Frosty says. "They were like two peas in a pod, and they became close."

Jack Miller, then vice president at Good Samaritan Hospital, provided a room in one of the houses near the hospital, allowing Joan and Connie to start planning and developing what became Hospice House in Hillsdale.

"Mom was one of the first to assist Joan, and then Mom recruited me, and you never say no to Mom and, later Joan," Frosty says.

He volunteered to write policies and procedures for the State Board of Health and the Oregon Board of Pharmacy, since the new facility didn't fit the regulations the state had for hospitals and nursing homes.

Frosty joined the board of directors for Hospice House, devoting 15 to 20 hours a week to the cause.

"I didn't want to see families in a situation where they can't care for their own," Frosty says. "They need clinical and psychological help as well as respite. And what if someone is by himself or herself? You need a specific in-patient hospice facility for them to spend the last days of their life that is cheaper than a hospital and much more high-touch than a nursing home."

Joan had raised money from the Fred Meyer Foundation and the Henningsen Family Foundation to purchase and remodel a facility on five acres of land in the west hills of Portland. It was to be the site for

FROSTY'S NO SNOWMAN

the first in-patient hospice facility in the U.S.

"We opened in September 1987 with $500,000 in the bank and no insurance provider contracts," Frosty says. "Our first patient was a 27-year- old Oregon Medicaid patient who was dying of ovarian cancer and had no money. You could not get Medicare accreditation unless you had a home hospice program. There were three or four very good home hospice programs already in the city; another one would have been duplicative.

"We had no way of billing and collecting from Medicaid, Medicare or any other health insurance. The challenge became, 'How do we operate on a cash basis?' "

Henningsen Cold Storage donated half the value of the property of the family patriarch, a large Tudor home on five acres in Hillsdale, a neighborhood in southwest Portland. The Hospice House board raised about a half-million dollars from foundations like Fred Meyer, Collins and Murdoch to pay for the rest of the property, to build a 15-bed in-patient facility attachment to the home, and to remodel and upgrade the old house. "When completed," Frosty says, "it was fantastic."

When Hospice House opened, it hosted a national hospice conference in Portland.

"Reviews across the country were overwhelmingly positive," Frosty says. "It opened a better understanding that you can't just do everything at home, in the hospital or the nursing home."

Throughout the next three years, Hospice House administrators staged several fund-raising events, such as golf tournaments and fashion shows. They wrote grants and got a warm reception from the city's charitable foundations.

Funding was always a problem, though. By 1990, Frosty was president of the board of directors for Hospice House.

"We were getting to the point where it became more difficult to finance it by raising money," he says.

"We tried to become an accredited entity with Medicare, but the requirements were onerous."

With all their efforts of fund-raising and church donations, Hospice House administrators found they did not have the infrastructure to operate it. After running the program with paid staff, a very active board of directors and several major fund-raising events and grants, the board wrote a request for proposal (RFP) for a group to take over the operations and continue the Hospice House mission.

Operations at Hospice House were suspended in December 1990. In March of 1991, there were many suitors for what was a prize piece of property in the west hills of Portland. They accepted a bid from Ecumenical Ministries of Oregon, who renamed it "Hopewell House."

"It was a consortium of a large number of Christian denominations with an affiliation with the Jewish community," Frosty says. "They found Hopewell House to be in their mission."

John Castles, whose business was raising investment capital for growth companies in the Northwest, was instrumental in funding what would be called Hopewell House. Castles is a senior trustee at the Murdock Foundation, a large private foundation created by the will of Jack Murdock, the co-founder of Tektronix, the first high technology company in the Northwest following World War II. The Murdock Trust, a multi-billion-dollar private foundation that serves five states of the Northwest, was created in 1975 following Jack's death.

"I give Frosty credit for getting me interested," Castles says. "He was an insider. He introduced me to Hopewell House. It became personal for me."

John's father, Jim Castles, was diagnosed with terminal stomach cancer and heart disease. He lived the last stages of his life in Hopewell House.

"It was a comfortable, private, familiar setting with excellent patient care and valuable and unique service," John says.

In 1995, the facility was taken over by Legacy Healthcare, headed by Bob Pallari.

"They accepted the responsibility to staff and operate it, because it gave them something they owned," Frosty says. "And it was an opportunity to get dying patients out of the hospital into a high-touch, high-tech in-patient hospice."

"When Hopewell House wanted to repurchase the facility, we were asked if it was something Murdock would help with," Castle says. "We said yes, definitely. The Friends of Hopewell House provided the Murdock foundation with a proposal and we gave a large grant toward the project — something in the $500,000 to $700,000 range." Legacy operated Hopewell House until it closed in 2019 and put the facility up for sale. A group called "Friends of Hopewell House" raised close to $5 million to get it operating again as a non-profit in January 2023.

"It's fantastic," Frosty says. "It's a service that the Portland area needs. I'm so glad Friends of Hopewell House were able to find the passion Portland still has for it and it is able to reopen."

❄

Many pharmacies are hit with drug diversion and theft problems. Good Sam was no exception during the Comer era.

"One of most egregious ones was when an ICU nurse was diverting morphine for her own use," Frosty says. "She would substitute tap water into an injectable morphine syringe, then use the morphine on herself."

FROSTY'S NO SNOWMAN

And: "An OB nurse's mother was dying of cancer. She was having to take care of her mother as well as being an assistant head nurse, and she started using the mother's Demerol. To supplement that, she started stealing from the nursing station supply."

When such violations occur, employees are fired and reported to their respective Oregon licensing boards for further review and discipline, which could range from license suspension to the requirement of entry into a diversion program. In the case of drug theft leading to selling or distribution, fines, arrests and incarcerations were possible.

During the '80s, stolen cocaine started showing up at parties — cocaine flakes that were used as an anesthetic in nose and throat surgeries.

"We had to develop a rigid narcotic control system," Frosty says. "We conducted a number of investigations when discrepancies were found. Nurses did an inventory after every shift. We would go in and dust some of the controlled substance containers. If someone started showing up with purple hands, you knew they had been dipping into the narcotics at the wrong time. We had to harden the target. We had some instances where nurses and physicians were forging prescriptions. We had to secure the prescription pads."

Some of the crimes were serious.

"One Saturday afternoon, we had a guy come into the out-patient pharmacy at Good Sam," Frosty says. "The perp was able to get into the waiting room, lock the door from the inside, jump over the counter, bind and gag the female pharmacist and walk out the door with every controlled substance we had.

"One night in 1984, we had a robbery by three men at Good Sam who broke into our inpatient pharmacy in the middle of the night. We were doing some construction in the pharmacy and the door that gave them entry was locked on the inside. The three guys called the elevators to the basement and disabled them. They tied up and gagged the hospital operators. They went in with guns, tied up pharmacy and pharmacy tech employees and took a half-million dollars' worth of controlled substances. The police never found them."

Today, security systems in hospitals are much improved, "but it's still an issue," Frosty says. "We had PRN (pharmacy recovery network), a rehab and diversion program for pharmacists who have had substance abuse problems. When I first started in pharmacy, it was very common for pharmacists, doctors and nurses to succumb to temptation. Some went over the edge and abused it. It is something everybody has to be aware of. We improved the necessary security systems, so it doesn't happen as often today."

Good Samaritan Hospital, Portland, Oregon

CHAPTER 7

Championing Vital Choice and Learning How To Thrive On Chaos

By the mid-to-late 1980s, things were changing quickly in the health care industry, throughout the country and especially in Portland.

Good Samaritan Hospital and Medical Center had gone from a 539-bed tertiary (specialty care) hospital to a 175-bed hospital. Medicare, followed by other insurance companies, had changed the way it reimbursed hospitals from a cost-based reimbursement to a diagnosis related groups (DRGs) system.

Medicare changed from paying the costs of what the hospitals reported/charged to a "fixed amount" based on the patient's diagnosis. Departments such as pharmacy, lab and radiology went from revenue-producing departments to cost centers that had to have very tight financial controls.

In pharmacy, drug information, medication formulary management, automation and the need for documented cost-effective outcomes became critically important. In the late 1970s and early '80s, the pharmacy department had already developed a home IV therapy program, implemented a robust cost-effective generic and therapeutic medication formulary management program, centralized much of the medication, IV dispensing and IV pumps and tubing and moved several pharmacists into the patient care areas where they could ensure the best drug information, compliance and pharmacy outcomes.

Good Samaritan was one of the first hospitals to meet the challenges of the Medicare's DRG program. The average length of stay for hospitalized patient had dropped from nine days in 1983 to about five in 1988. Because of decreased inpatient revenue due to the decline of hospitalized patients, however, there were major layoffs in the hospital and to the pharmacy staff in 1989.

Prior to the layoffs, Comer had been thriving. In the summer of 1988, Frosty was one of a small group of Good Sam employees nominated for employee of the year. In the spring of 1989, he was selected Hospital Pharmacist of the Year by the Oregon Society of Hospital Pharmacists.

In November 1988, he was laid off.

"I was absolutely shocked," Comer says. "I was responsible for planning, development, implementation and maintenance of all the operations for Good Sam's pharmacy department of about 120 employees. I led the team that developed the home IV therapy program, which was by this time making about $1 million a year; the outpatient pharmacy, which was growing; a new two-nursing home pharmacy program when Good Sam purchased the facilities, and the operations of a very busy inpatient pharmacy.

"I understood because of financial considerations that we had to cut back," Frosty says. "I truly believe, though, that I shouldn't have been laid off. I'd done a good job. I was getting good reviews. We were also managing the pharmacy benefits for 3,000 hospital employees.

"The thing that hurt the most was being part of the change agents that shepherded Good Sam through the chaos of DRGs. As it turned out, it was the best thing that ever happened to me, though I didn't know it at the time."

After news of the layoff broke, Frosty says, "I was approached by a number of friends in the pharmacy business, saying, 'Come work for us.' But I wanted to complete all the projects I had been responsible for at Good Sam. After being told I was laid off the Monday before Thanksgiving 1988, I was asked to stay until February 28, 1989 to complete the specific projects."

The next year, Legacy Health was formed with the merger of Good Sam, Emanuel, Meridian Park, Physician and Surgeon, Holladay Park and Mount Hood Medical Center Hospitals.

The timing was bad. Vicki had gone to work in 1980 as an administrative assistant for Ponderosa Enterprise, a subsidiary of Far West Federal Bank that handled construction and maintenance of their banks throughout Oregon. She also worked in accounting for another subsidiary, Greentree. In 1989, Far West sold to another bank and Vicki's position was eliminated.

After his layoff in November, Frosty was given six months' severance that started March 1, 1989, plus paid employment counseling. After the latter, he took an aptitude test. "The best fit for my next job? A hospital administrator," he says with a laugh.

Frosty stayed on at Good Sam until the end of February 1989. In the interim, he had been contacted by representatives of Vital Care, a national home infusion therapy company.

Out of the interview process came an offer for Frosty to serve as president and general manager of a new Oregon branch. He accepted it, beginning in April 1989. First, though, he took a month of unemployment in March. With the $600, he bought a foosball table that he put in a room off of his garage.

"It's still there," Frosty says.

From the end of November, 1988 to the end of February 1989,

while working to finish the projects the hospital needed, he started planning and implementing the new Oregon Vital Care branch. He found a location for the new Vital Care office and got the pharmacy equipped, staffed and licensed in September 1989.

"I then became a health care administrator," Frosty says. "All the experience I had in the hospital industry, both in the military and my civilian life, started to pay off and gave me more confidence. Because Good Sam had given Jim Sanger and me the opportunity to be all we could be by implementing new and different things to reduce cost, improve outcomes, and income, I had been through a lot of change."

Frosty became inspired by a book on the challenges of staying relevant in business, Tom Peters' "Thriving on Chaos."

"I had started looking for property for an office and made arrangements for supplies and equipment for my own branch's business," Frosty says. "I'd never thought of myself as an entrepreneur, but it turned out I was. Peters talked about opportunities — 'Is your cup half empty or is it half full?' Suddenly, a light went on. From that point, every time something negative happened, I was able to turn it into a positive.

"Looking back, the summary of my pharmacy career was being more entrepreneurial and not being afraid to create new paradigms. Don't be afraid to take risks. Look for opportunities. Look for the voids that desperately need to be filled."

❄

The location for the new Vital Care office in Portland was on Northwest Front Street under the Fremont Bridge on the west side of the Willamette River.

"It was a great location," Frosty says. "Being next to the river gave us a place to wind down after a busy day and, occasionally, Mike Quaranta, my good friend and outpatient pharmacy supervisor at Good Sam, would bring his ski boat to the dock and we'd go water skiing during lunch."

Pharmacist Paulette Egging and pharmacy technician Steve Tillery joined Frosty as partners of the business. Jeannine Sumption, from Good Samaritan Health Enterprises, became the office manager and Milt Lehman the business manager. Jane Urban, from Oregon Health Sciences University, was hired as IV nurse.

"That was the starting six," Frosty says.

For nine months, the Portland office was a branch of Vital Care. Its corporate entity was an oil and coal company on the stock exchange in Canada.

"They had no interest in the clinical component," Frosty says. "It was the worst environment. Their idea was, 'Grow the market share, then turn and burn,' like flipping houses. I was spending a third of my time fending off vendors and trying to get Vital Care's CEO, Jim Rash, to pay bills. They were covering salaries, but they were not paying our offices expenses and vendor's bills."

In early 1990, Comer's group formed its own company. It cost them between $40,000 and $50,000 to assume the assets and liabilities of Vital Care, and they changed the name to "Vital Choice."

"Vicki had just gotten laid off from Far West Federal Bank," Frosty says. "Both my partners were going through divorces and had no money and our two daughters were in college at OSU."

Frosty took out a $40,000 loan from Jay and Linda Johnson. Jay and Frosty had been volunteers on the Mount Hood Ski Patrol. Linda was Vicki's best friend. The couples shared a cabin in Rhododendron on the mountain, along with Frosty's sister, Casey, and her husband, Ned.

"Vicki and I put our house up as collateral for the bridge loan," Frosty says. "And Milt and I hit the streets looking for investors. We were selling ourselves. Paulette was a great clinician, but at the time wasn't the one to ask investors for money. Milt was a wizard with spread sheets, and brilliant as a financial guy. The three of us were able to put together a good partnership that complemented each other's strengths with a great business plan."

Among the first potential investors Frosty and Milt met with was John Kinsman, who served on the board of directors of Hospice House with Frosty, when he was the board president. During the meeting, Frosty asked Kinsman for $50,000 to be a primary investor and to help recruit other investors.

"He took out his checkbook, wrote a check for $50,000 and handed it to me on the spot," Frosty says. "That hit me hard, that someone of John's financial acumen trusted me enough to get us started.
"It also created significant stress and concern about what would happen to my family if we fail, since I felt I was the partner that was on the hook for the loans and investors' expectations. Vicki and I would lose our home and we couldn't afford to have Wendy and Molly go to college. Seeing the girls 'flipping burgers' wasn't going to happen, if I could help it." Comer and Lehman also got a considerable investment from Jim Castles and his son, John, the latter whose business was raising investment capital for growth companies in the Northwest. He was also chairman of Oregon Salmon, for which his company had done a leverage buyout.

"I well recall my first meeting with Frosty," says Castles, a graduate of Beaverton's Sunset High and the University of Washington. "He and Milt called on me. I was the most active 'angel investor' in Oregon at the time, helping secure venture financing for growth companies and helping start-up companies start with individual investors.

"When they pitched me on the business concept for Vital Choice,

I was immediately impressed with the market potential and with the management expertise of both of them. I felt Milt covered the business and finance side, and Frosty covered the pharmaceutical and operations side of the business. I agreed to help raise capital and take a board seat."

Castles would later become executive chairman of Vital Choice.

"I went to the office every day and had an active management role," he says. "We grew the company, wrote a business plan together."

Castles was intrigued with Vital Choice's pursuit "of a business line for the comfort, privacy and safety of patients in their own home as opposed to receiving IV treatments in the hospital at enormous cost."

"In 1988, the cost for hospital overnight treatment was about $5,000 to $10,000 a day," he says. "The key to the business was third-party insurance reimbursements for payments to receive treatments. There were phenomenal advantages. Patients didn't have to drive from their home, so it was convenient. There was privacy and confidentiality and experienced pharmacists and nurses available, on call 24 hours a day, every day. And it was far less expensive for what they had to pay for hospital visits or having a long hospital stay for just IV therapies. The economic side was sound.

"There are some similarities between Vital Choice and Hopewell House in terms of uniqueness of services provided. Together, we had a team effort in terms of managing and growing Vital Choice into the success it became, and also a great investment."

Comer refers to Castles as his "angel mentor;" John views it more that they were colleagues and business partners.

"Frosty is a force of personality, and I mean that in a friendly way," Castles says. "He is a high-energy go-getter. He is like a pit bull with a bone in his teeth. When he latches onto something, he doesn't let go.

He is driven and passionate about the mission and purpose of an organization. He is dogged in his pursuit of excellence."

Preston Wilson, a senior health care executive with experience in national health care organizations, was hired as Vital Choice's CEO.

"Paulette Egging and Frosty oversaw the pharmacy and nursing staff," Castles says. "Frosty was a great team player. As a retired Colonel and pharmacy officer in the Army, he exemplified leadership skills and experience second to none. He learned a great deal from the structure and formality of the military roles he played. He came to have good administrative and leadership skills. He was a quick learner."

Castles came to admire Comer for both his business savvy and ethics and calls him a "visionary."

"I want to emphasize this: Frosty agreed with my personal business philosophy," Castles says. "That is to always do the right thing for your customers and for your shareholders. He displays high ethical standards and moral compass.

"I give Frosty credit as someone very active in capital formation of private and start-up companies, particularly in Oregon. I have worked with a lot of founders and CEOs of organizations. The good founders know what they know and know what they don't know. Founders typically have a lot of blind spots in terms of self-awareness. Frosty's feet are planted firmly on the ground. He had definite ideas about how to provide exceptional customer service. We always wanted to exceed our customers' expectations. All of us were aligned in these important principles and business philosophies. There was no acrimony. It was a well-oiled machine that worked very efficiently together. I credit Frosty and the others involved.

"Frosty was patient and just a solid guy all-around. He gets things done. He is a highly principled, strong-minded individual, yet willing to learn and willing to be a good listener and learn from others. That's somewhat rare in today's world."

A close friend of Castles' gifted him with a Russian-made military-style watch.

"When Frosty was called up to the Gulf War, I gave that to him," Castles says. "I have no idea to the value is, but that was not important. I wanted Frosty to remember us in Portland while we prayed for him to stay safe with the call-up. That watch was a memento of my respect and appreciation for Frosty."

Alas, it is gone.

"I lost it," Frosty says. "I wore it. It was so cool. But I don't know what happened to it. It probably got lost in the packing and repacking of our duffel bags during our deployment. It was definitely something I treasured, especially because it was a gift from John."

❄

Vital Choice added other investors and, beginning in February 1990, the business was off and running, with Frosty as president and Milt and Paulette as vice presidents. They hired another full-time nurse and part-time technicians and pharmacists and began to grow.

Frosty was learning how to run a company.

"One of the best lessons I learned of what not to do as a manager was from my second boss at Good Sam, Marilyn Slotfeldt," Frosty says. "It was her management style, which I dubbed the totem pole style of management, where you could find yourself at the top of the pole one minute and the bottom the next.

"She was bright, an excellent writer and could have been a great defense or prosecuting attorney. We would have two-to-three-hour management meetings on Monday; she would praise you in front of all the managers one minute and then tear you down the next, depending on what your response would be to an issue."

Frosty found himself trying to guess what Slotfeldt wanted instead of offering his opinion and backing it up as best he could. But he learned how to write better, how to organize arguments and proposals.

"I promised myself never to compromise like that again and to give my best argument, back it up and, if I'm wrong, admit it and learn from it," he says. "Don't ever compromise your principles to someone who is playing games for their pleasure.

"Marilyn was the opposite of Jim Sanger. He would say, 'Let's do it, and we'll ask for resources or forgiveness later.' Marilyn would say, 'We have to dot every 'I' and cross every 'T.' We must write a proposal that will knock their socks off before we do anything.' Jim was far better working with people. Marilyn was a brilliant writer, but was what I later called an 'academically constrained entrepreneur.'" During their time together at Good Samaritan, Frosty and Paulette pioneered another program.

"In 1979, we started doing hyperalimentation (total parenteral nutrition/TPN)," Sanger says. "When, for whatever reason, the patients weren't getting sufficient nutrition to live and couldn't be fed by mouth, they would be admitted to Good Sam. They would be fed via a central IV catheter with usually a two-liter bag of amino acids, Dextrose, lipids, vitamins and minerals over an eight-hour period."

Paulette wrote the first manual for the delivery of hyperalimentation in collaboration with Dr. Mike Hartnett. Frosty was the assistant director of operations when the program was implemented.

"When he left Good Sam," Sanger says, "he and Paulette used a lot of the things they had learned at Good Sam."

❄

Meanwhile, Vicki Comer was back to work.

"I didn't get a job right away," she says. "Molly, our younger daughter, was a senior in high school. I was in charge of the all-night graduation party. I wanted to have those last six months with her. I was having fun. I learned to play golf.

"One day, Frosty said, 'I think you should go into real estate, especially if our home IV therapy company should fail.' I said, 'You've got to be kidding. I'm not made out to be a salesperson working on commission.'" "Your friends think you would be good at it," Frosty responded.

They were persuasive. Vicki attended classes at the Real Estate School of Oregon and, in July 1990, passed her examinations, both state and federal. In October, she started with Lutz Snyder Realty. The office was located a mile from the Comers' home in the Sexton Mountain section of Beaverton.

By this time, the Comer girls were growing up.

"They were wicked smart and very active in several sports," Frosty says.

Wendy was 20 and had just completed her sophomore year at Oregon State. Molly, 18, had just graduated from Beaverton High and was heading to Oregon State to join her sister. Born in Vicenza, Italy, when Frosty was on active duty and just 16 months apart, they were close growing up. Was Wendy tough on her younger sibling?

"She says she was provoked," Molly says with a chuckle, "but she was the one doing the provoking."

"Actually, I think the roles were reversed," Wendy says. "We argued all the time but really, we got along pretty well."

Wendy participated in many sports, including soccer, basketball and softball. She played second base in the latter.

"I like team sports and the camaraderie of it," she says. "It was fun to play in high school."

Molly was even more involved.

"The focus for me in high school was sports," she says. "Play anything and every sport possible. I played basketball and softball and I skied. Wendy and I ski raced in high school. With our place in Rhododendron, we would go up pretty much every weekend until right before we got into high school.

"But soccer was my love, my passion. All my best friends played. I love the creativity of the game. And there's a lot of running involved, which I liked. You have to be in shape."

As a senior in 1990, Molly was named Metro League Player of the Year. She was first-team all-state and runner-up to Hillsboro's Tiffany Milbrett as Oregon's Player of the Year. Milbrett won an Olympic gold medal in 1996 and the 1999 World Cup as a member of the U.S. national team and has been inducted into the National Soccer Hall of Fame.

"Tiffany was a good friend of mine," Molly says. "Getting Metro League Player of the Year wasn't deserved. It may have been that Tiffany had gotten so many awards, voters decided to give it to someone else. She was an offensive player and I was more all-around, but she was so dominant, it didn't make sense to me."

A little more than a year after Vital Choice was founded, Saddam Hussein invaded Kuwait. Frosty Comer's life was in for a big change.

Above: LTC Tony Angello, MD, & Vicki promoting Frosty to Captain, Vicenza, Italy, 1970

Left: Clayton Comer & Frosty, Vicenza, Italy, 1970

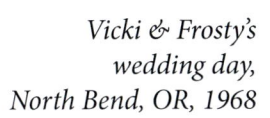

Vicki & Frosty's wedding day, North Bend, OR, 1968

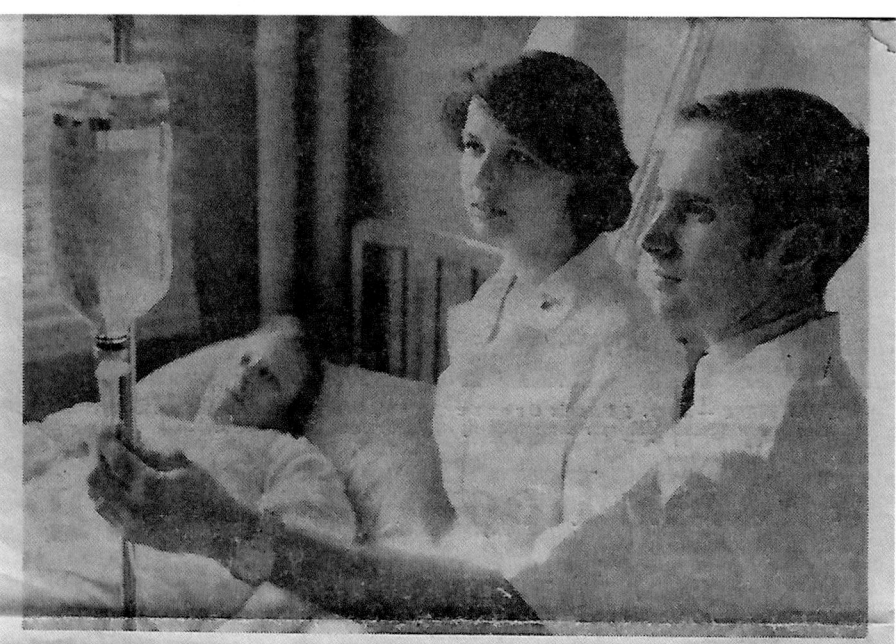

UNIT-DOSE SYSTEM—Capt. William F. Comer, head of the Vicenza Hospital pharmacy, adds drug to IV solution as nurse Capt. Marilyn M. Rees and patient T. Sgt. Robert E. Douglas look on. The system lightens the load of often-overworked nurses. —S&S, Grandy

Stars & Stripes August 1971

Pharmacists Prepare Medicines At Army Hospital in Vicenza

By BOB HOYER
Mediterranean Bureau

VICENZA, Italy (S&S) — To most patients medicine is medicine and they don't care who prepares it as long as they get what the doctor ordered.

But hospital pharmacists trained under a new system of preparing medicants take a different view.

For a number of reasons they prefer to prepare the prescriptions themselves — rather than tie up the nurse on the ward with this pharmaceutical duty.

Relatively new in the field of pharmacy, the unit-dose system of preparing daily inpatient prescriptions has been adopted by a number of civilian and military hospitals in the United States.

The first hospital in Europe to switch to the system was the U.S. Army hospital in Vicenza, which early this year added a centralized additive system for intravenous (IV) preparations.

"The big advantage of these centralized systems is that the nurse is relieved of much of her pharmaceutical work load, and is free to concentrate on other duties," said hospital chief pharmacist Capt. William F. Comer.

"Under this new setup pharmacy personnel (Comer is assisted by five enlisted men — two of whom are registered pharmacists) get the medical orders from doctors for all patients.

"The job of getting the orders, preparing the medicine and putting unit doses back on the wards now is the responsibility of the pharmacy," Comer said.

"Under the old system, the nurse would order bulk medicines from us and keep a small pharmacy on the ward.

"Now ward stock has been reduced by two-thirds. With this system there is less chance of medicine going out-of-date."

Comer pointed out that under the unit-dose plan, all individual doses are prepared in sanitary plastic envelopes.

"By taking drugs off the nurse's station and putting them back in the pharmacy we have relieved the nurse of the extra book work now required on all control drugs," Comer said.

"Under the Bureau of Narcotics Act of 1970, drugs fall into three classifications — Code K (depressants and stimulants), regular and narcotics. Control drugs now require at least 10 per cent more paperwork."

Comer pointed out that another advantage of unit dose is that it permits the pharmacy to keep tighter control of its inventory.

Under the old intravenous system, the nurse on the ward mixed IV fluids. Now, pharmacists go to the ward to do mixing, which includes such additives as vitamins, antibiotics, hormones, steroids, etc.

It takes one to two hours every morning to make unit-dose preparations and complete IV mixing orders for a 24-hour period.

"We then check in the afternoons to see what additional orders doctors have made," Comer said.

What do nurses think of the system?

"There was some resistance. Whenever you change a system, it's natural to expect some opposition.

"But I think we have demonstrated and proved the advantages of the new centralized systems," Comer pointed out.

Vicenza nurse Capt. Marilyn M. Rees seemed to agree with Comer's appraisal.

"The new system really is an improvement. Nurses here do have a busy work schedule and work being done by the pharmacists saves us time," she said.

Comer gave a briefing on the unit dose system to the 1971 USAREUR pharmacy conference in Berlin.

Clayton, Vicki and BG Maroney, Commander of Madigan Army Medical Center, awarding Frosty the Army Commendation Medal, 1973.

Captain Frosty Comer & SP5 John Pack working in the 45th Field Hospital Pharmacy, Vicenza, Italy, 1970.

Frosty at bat for 45th Field Hoospital softball team, Vicenza, Italy, 1971.

t: Captains Frost Comer & Marily Rees, Stars & ipes article, 45th Field spital, Vicenza, Italy, 71.

Curly & Connie Leininger with Bill & Connie Comer at Vicki & Frosty's wedding, May 18, 1968, North Bend, OR.

Frosty Comer, 1968

Vicki Comer, 1968.

Kim Comer, 1974.

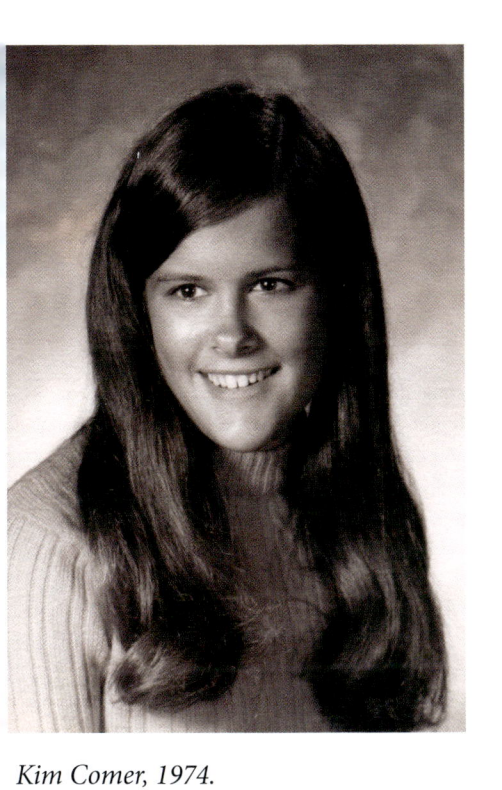

Molly & Wendy Comer, 1974.

Frosty & Jim Sanger at Good Samaritan Hospital Pharmacy, 1976.

Casey, Connie, Kim & Frosty at Lake Chelan, WA, 1980.

Connie Comer, 1972.

Mike Quaranta & Frosty, skiing on Mt. Bachelor, OR, 1989.

Molly & Wendy Comer, Highland Junior High School, 1984.

Frosty with his 45th Station Hospital Pharmacy staff, Ft. Lewis, WA preparing for Desert Storm deployment, 1990.

Left: MAJ Dennis Rogers, LTC Cab Clark & LTC Frosty Comer at Ft. Lewis, WA preparing for deployment to Desert Storm, Dec. 23, 1990.

Hopewell House, Portland, Oregon, 2023

Above: MAJ Mike Roggi, Assistant Chief, Pharmacy, 5th General Orthopedic Hospital, Stuttgart Germany, 1991.

Above: Pharmacy staff with Frosty, 5th General Orthopedic Hospital, Stuttgart, Germany, 1991.

Right: Frosty with LTG General & wife before Dressage ride, 1991.

CHAPTER 8

BRIDGING THE GULF

In November 1990, soldiers began getting called up for active duty throughout the U.S., including those stationed at the 45th Station Hospital in Vancouver, Wash. Operation Desert Shield/Storm was on. It was the first such Military Reserve and National Guard deployment since the Korean War (1950-53).

Frosty Comer had essentially been in the military since 1968, with 4 1/2 years of active duty during the Vietnam War and in the active Army Reserves ranks from 1973-90. He had first been commissioned as a first lieutenant, promoted to captain in 1970, then transferred to the Army Reserves in 1973. Ten years later, he was promoted to major, then to lieutenant colonel in 1988. That was his rank in 1990 when the U.S. Army came calling again. (He would be promoted again to his final rank of colonel in 1993).

"I had trained at several medical centers," Frosty says. "We had done field training and mass casualty exercises, and I had been on active duty in medical support of active-duty troops. I completed my three-year advanced officer course along with three years of command and general staff college. I was ready."

Frosty had to leave his civilian job at Vital Choice with no idea of when he might be able to return, depending on the length and outcome of the first Gulf War.

"Luckily, I had two good partners," he says. "We hired Gary Schnabel to fill my position while I was gone. Gary had been a pharmacy manager of an Option Care franchise in Eugene and was also a nurse. He later became the executive director of the Oregon Board of Pharmacy."

Frosty reported to the 45th Station Hospital for deployment at Fort Vancouver barracks in November 1990.

The mission was to backfill and augment medical units in Europe.

"Our unit had the right medical specialties in the right slots," Frosty says. "We were ready to be deployed in one week. The DOD (Department of Defense) wanted 20 of our nurses to go to Saudi Arabia. We were equipment poor, but people rich."

Frosty was deployed to Germany with the 450-person 45th Station Hospital unit. When he arrived at his assigned hospital in Germany, he replaced Captain Ken Dick, who was the chief of pharmacy at the 5th General Hospital in Stuttgart. Captain Dick had been recently mobilized with a combat support hospital to Saudi Arabia.

The two weeks before Christmas, Frosty and the rest of the 45th Station Hospital personnel took a bus from Portland to Fort Lewis, Wash., to join other soldiers in barracks preparing for active duty. Frosty's unit flew on Christmas Eve, on a Tower Air Charter 747 to New York and then to Frankfurt.

"It was kind of like Santa Claus flying over the North Pole," Frosty recalls. "We passed out candies and gifts on the plane, and then we slept. We landed in Frankfurt on Christmas Day. Upon arriving at the unit assignment center, the active duty staff started calling out each clinical section and designated to which hospital unit and city the individual soldier would be assigned.

"Instead of working as a whole hospital unit, we were being 'cannibalized' and sent to medical units throughout Europe that needed specific clinical personnel. I would love to have gone to Vicenza (Italy), but I was sent to Stuttgart."

Comer flew to Europe with two pharmacy officers with whom he had served in Army Reserves at Fort Vancouver — Cab Clark and Dennis Rogers. Clark was among the reservists sent to Fort Lewis for deployment.

"We had known each other from Fort Vancouver, but the training at Fort Lewis really started our relationship," Clark says.

Clark was assigned as the Chief of Pharmacy at the 45th Field Hospital in Vicenza, Italy — the place Frosty had served nearly 20 years earlier. And Dennis Rogers was sent to Berlin.

"Because Dennis was a Major and Cab was a new Lieutenant Colonel whose pharmacy practice was in the retail world, they were sent to smaller units," Frosty says. "I was sent to a specialty orthopedic hospital as a more senior Lieutenant Colonel, since I had extensive military and civilian hospital experience."

Rogers, today a retired Lieutenant Colonel pharmacy officer, spent 32 years in the Army. He also worked in retail pharmacies and hospitals as well as for insurance companies as a pharmacy manager.

"Our generation of active reserve pharmacy officers were always available to take an assignment when the Army was to go somewhere," Rogers says. "This time, we backfilled the hospitals in Germany and Italy while all their regular active-duty folks went to the Gulf."

Rogers recalls that Frosty "really liked" Stuttgart.

"They put the officers in an off-site hotel," Rogers recalls. "He liked that because the Lufthansa stewardesses would stay there, and the pool was what they called 'textile frei' — no clothes. Frosty enjoyed that."

Rogers, who now lives in Brasada Ranch in central Oregon, has maintained a friendship with Comer through the years.

"Frosty is a guy who likes to keep busy," Rogers says. "He is into all sorts of things. He has to be involved in just about anything that goes on. He is a doer; he gets things done. And he is an entrepreneur."

Rogers attended the University of Oregon and got an undergraduate degree in chemistry. Later, he spent 3 1/2 years in Corvallis gaining his degree in pharmacy at Oregon State.

To Frosty and Vicki Comer, that means he should be a Beaver sports fan.

"Frosty has always kidded me about this, and Vicki is on me all the time," Rogers says. "He always gets on me because I'm a Duck fan. Really, you might call me a platypus. I'll root for the Beavers if they're not playing the Ducks, but if they are playing each other, no way."

❄

The 5th General Hospital in Stuttgart was given an impossible assignment by the European Medical Command in Heidelberg, Germany.

"We were told to expect 10,000 casualties a day to hit the European theater hospitals," Frosty says. "The evacuation route for casualties was from the Gulf to Europe."

Five German cities were designated as "centers of excellence." Stuttgart was for orthopedics. The other centers, with different specialties, were in Munich, Berlin, Frankfurt and Heidelberg.

"We knew Iraq had chemical weapons," Frosty says. "Saddam Hussein had been gassing the Kurds. I was getting secret messages about what antibiotics to stock; we were told to anticipate that our troops could be attacked with Anthrax."

When he had been in Vicenza in the early '70s, Frosty had NATO secret clearance.

"One of my extra duties, I was a secret document officer for the hospital," he says. "I had a Sergeant First Class (E7) who reported to me. He and I were responsible for all the secret documents that were sent to the 45th Field Hospital in the Southern Europe Task Force (SETAF), which was established during World War II.

"The military divided up areas that commands are responsible for. We had responsibility for the Mediterranean area. Every week, you are getting some kind of secret documents from the U.S. Department of Defense. They would also be sending those to forces in Spain and Italy. It was more nerve-racking than controlling narcotics. Both will get you court-marshaled and sent to jail, especially if you mishandle or lose a secret document."

In Stuttgart, Frosty's secret clearance had to be re-established. In the meantime, he had plenty of duties.

"In order to protect civilians and military personnel, we had to know what we needed to stock, such as appropriate amounts of Atropine (nerve agents) and antibiotics that would treat Anthrax or other biological agents," he says. "I became part of the hospital command structure, planning for 10,000 casualties a day out of the Gulf."

The U.S. sent more than 500,000 troops to the Persian Gulf for Operation Desert Shield/Storm. It became the largest air campaign since the conflict in Southeast Asia in the 1960s and early '70s.

"We were facing the fifth largest army in the world (Iraq)," Frosty says. "But we wiped them out in five days."

Frosty's roommate in Stuttgart was Dr. Jeff Bert, an orthopedic surgeon from Coos Bay, Oregon. He became the chief of orthopedic medicine at the Fifth General hospital in Bad Cannstatt, Stuttgart.

"We were tasked to be a 600-bed hospital in this World War II German hospital that had only 100 functional beds with the appropriate up to-date electricity and equipment," Frosty recalls. "There were an additional 200 beds that were non-functional and didn't have the electrical infrastructure to support a light bulb, let alone an IV pump or respirator. You could barely turn the lights on."

When Dr. Bert arrived, there wasn't enough orthopedic equipment, either.

"At the time we arrived on Christmas night 1990, there was only enough orthopedic equipment to outfit one patient in bed," Frosty says.

Frosty was given charge of the hospital's lab and X-ray department as well as the inpatient and outpatient pharmacies. He met the next morning with the hospital's executive staff and commander to start planning how they were going to become a 600-bed orthopedic specialty hospital. They were nowhere near ready to receive orthopedic casualties. Dr. Bert ordered more than $4 million in orthopedic equipment and Frosty ordered more than $1 million in pharmaceuticals and IV solutions.

Within a month, the U.S. military paid for the Germans to upgrade the 200-bed wing of the hospital to the standards required to support electrical, plumbing and basic medical needs.

"That gave us a grand total of 300 beds," Frosty says. "That didn't get us to 600, but it was a start. The U.S. government spent millions of dollars improving this German hospital from dilapidated World War II structure to minimal 1990 standards. But we still didn't meet the medical command's requirement for 600 beds with a 30-day length-of-stay assumption."

At one of the 5th General Hospital's executive planning session, Frosty offered a proposal to the commander, which he hoped would solve the number of beds and length-of-stay assumptions. Not surprisingly, Frosty drew upon his Good Sam experience dealing with Medicare's new DRG program, that resulted in a reduced length-of-hospital stay and the need for fewer number of beds.

Frosty's proposal:

"Let's work with the local Red Cross to have a Job Fair, where we bring in American government civilians, military dependents — typically wives, but in some cases husbands — and any good English-speaking Germans for interview sessions to find what medical skill sets they have to assist in staffing."

Comer said there were many empty barracks near the hospital that could be used to house post-op orthopedic patients that only needed rehabilitation services and not acute care.

"These could be staffed with these volunteers supervised by active-duty medical personnel," he said.

Frosty was responsible for overseeing the operation with assistance from the hospital commander, chief nurse and the German Red Cross. They brought in 400 civilians for interviews. Out of that, they identified about 100 people capable of performing a number of functions, "from semi-acute to non-acute care," he says. "It was a beautiful experience. Everybody dropped what they were doing and came to see how they could help. The German volunteers were well-educated and great people."

Today, Comer is proud he was able to assist in the development of an alternative strategic plan for a major medical operation "that married the expertise and experience of the active duty and reserve medical component of our military."

"Since this was the first time the Reserves and National Guard had been mobilized since the Korean conflict, there was a lot of unknowns and anxiety about how these groups would work together and perform," Frosty says. "Because of the effort of our 45th Station Hospital soldiers, our unit was awarded a Presidential Citation.

"When I look back at my career, the message is, be accepting of things you may not want to do and learn from them. It may pay off in unique ways."

Because of Frosty recommendations, the European Army Medical Command in Heidelberg approved the change and allowed the 5th General Hospital to implement the plan. As a result of his input, Comer was given the Army Commendation (ARCOM) Award for meritorious service.

"Being plucked out of your home and civilian job, sent 7,000 miles away, dropped into a new environment and all of sudden you are able to contribute — that was self-actualizing for me," Frosty says.

❄

When the Fort Vancouver crew arrived in Stuttgart, there was already a National Guard unit from Tennessee and an Army Reserve unit from Utah on the premises. In January 1991 came a unit from Dallas that pulled from states around Texas, and one from Wisconsin. Major Mike Roggi, a pharmacy officer from the Wisconsin unit joined Frosty as his assistant Chief of Pharmacy. They are friends to this day.

"It was a melting pot from different regions, ethnicities, dialects and to some extent, cultures," Frosty recalls. "Lee Greenwood's song, 'God Bless the USA,' was our anthem besides the national anthem. The folks from Utah would probably be in bed sleeping by 10 p.m.; the folks from Tennessee would still be drinking at 11 p.m.

"What I think is so amazing about Americans, here you had people from all four corners of the U.S. It was the first time significant numbers of members of the Reserves and National Guard were called to duty since Korea. Civilian lives were disrupted unexpectedly, they were sent overseas, and now we had to work as a highly functional, clinical team. Within a month after everybody arrived, we had everybody in the right job and highly functional. Everybody was well-trained, knew what to do and knew how to work as a team."

Frosty will never forget watching Dick Cheney — then the U.S. Secretary of Defense — in January 1991 on TV before the war started.

"Thanks to the Reserves and National Guard for being ready, but I want to be straight with you," Cheney said. "You need to expect this is going to be a very long war. We know they have chemical and biological weapons, because they used them on the Iranians and Kurds. We don't know to what extent. You need to plan for being in your current location for one year and then rotate to another each year until we win this war."

"We looked at each and said, 'Holy crap. We're in this for a long time,'" Frosty says. "The example was Vietnam. How long did that last?"

Frosty worried about his new home IV therapy business in Portland.

"What the hell am I going to do?" he asked himself. "Am I going to lose my company? I had two partners, but I was the primary person, who had to do the marketing and get doctors, hospitals and insurance companies to refer patients to us."

Frosty quickly became engaged with the friendships he made and the diversity in the military.

"There was an amazing transition happening with Army Reserves women's involvement," he says. "In our civilian lives, while serving in the Reserves or National Guard, we had women who were majors, captains, lieutenant colonels, who were in charge of something for a weekend or two weeks of annual training. When they went home, many of them were wives, mothers and workers who went back to their civilian world.

"But I saw a number of women realizing, 'This is what I really want.' When the war was over so fast, some of them said, 'I don't want to leave.' These women did an amazing job and were serious about the new accountability and responsibility they had. They loved it. They weren't necessarily getting that satisfaction in their civilian lives. I'm sure some of them remained in the military on active duty."

During his 4 1/2 years of active duty service during the Vietnam war, Comer saw only one black non-commissioned officer or woman in any Army pharmacy capacity.

"Every member of my staff was a Caucasian male," he says. "When I landed in Stuttgart, I was the minority, one of two Caucasians in the pharmacy department. We had blacks and Puerto Ricans in various important positions. That showed me the military had truly educated and invested in people, regardless of their race or gender and it was refreshing to work in an eclectic fun environment."

As the hospital crew in Stuttgart waited weeks for the war to begin and casualties to arrive, they tended to soldiers with athletic or work-related injuries, "like somebody falling off a tank or playing basketball," Frosty says. "There were people who needed the tertiary care that Dr. Bert and the rest of us could provide. If someone tore his ACL, it had to be repaired quickly. They were worried if the war started, we'd be overwhelmed and wouldn't be able to take care of more serious casualties. But we needed practice working together, too. We got to a point where we were ready for any type of injury or casualty."

Frosty recalls one unusual injury: "A female military dependent was having an affair. She got caught in the bedroom by her husband, who had unexpectedly returned from Saudi Arabia, jumped out of the window, and suffered a compound fracture of her femur."

Dr. Jeff Bert admitted her to the hospital and, with the help of Frosty and two nurses, set her leg by drilling a rod through the tibia. He attached the traction apparatus to the rod and the stretching apparatus was attached to the bed.

"This took less than 15 minutes, under the sedation I provided, and immediately relieved her pain," Frosty says. "It's a great example of how staff from different units in our country could come together quickly and have a positive patient outcome. Dealing with her severe injury was easy for us. Her challenge was to deal with her husband."

The head of emergency medicine at the Oregon Health Sciences University, Dr. Donald Trunkey, served in Saudi Arabia. He would be awarded a Bronze star for his service in Desert Storm.

"He and General (Norman) Schwarzkopf went head-to-head about what kind of emergency health care was needed," Frosty says. "We needed to have our medical treatment and evacuation capabilities as close to the front lines as possible. Dr. Trunkey had to convinced General Schwarzkopf that it was safe for the Reserves to be a critical part of the initial triage and treatment staff of the Combat Support Hospitals, that were upgrades of the old MASH hospitals in Vietnam.

"The general attitude among the military leaders toward the Reserves and National Guard? They weren't sure how effective we could be. We were treated as second-class citizens, both in respect as well as simple things like billeting."

Very soon, though, at least some of those in charge found themselves impressed with the health care set-up in Stuttgart and other active duty medical settings.

※

General James McCarthy was a four-star Air Force general who was commander of the U.S. European Command and deputy commander of NATO during the Gulf War. He was headquartered in Stuttgart.

"The general's chief of staff had a very bad back," Frosty Comer recalls. "He was sent to us, and the general was impressed with the care he got from Dr. Bert."

Dr. Bert became the chief of orthopedic medicine at the Fifth General hospital in Bad Cannstatt. Bert and Frosty were roommates there and close friends.

When their hospital unit arrived in Stuttgart in December 1990, the waiting time for a doctor's appointment on the nine bases that were part of the American Stuttgart military complex was seven weeks.

"Because of our Reserve and National Guard medical units, within a week, we had the waiting time down to a day or less," Frosty says. "Wait time and the quality of care improved dramatically over the next month or two. The active-duty military and their dependents had not experienced this kind of care before, but hey, we were all in. We wanted this thing to end."

Within a month after arrival, the base medical crew was ready to accept as many casualties as possible in their 300-bed hospital.

General McCarthy's chief of staff was treated for a ruptured disc by Bert, "and it was so successful, General McCarthy wanted to meet with us," Frosty says.

They convened one Saturday night in late January 1991 at the Officer's Club at Patch Barracks, which had been General Eisenhower's headquarters during World War II.

"He wanted to know how all of us were doing," Frosty says. "He was so impressed with how much the health care services had improved. We spent two hours talking about why we were in the military, why we had volunteered to do this.

"The reason for the vast majority of us was the love of country, along with the travel, adventure and potential retirement benefits. In Jeff's case, he had an even greater potential sacrifice. He and his wife had five kids and went from making a lot of money as a full-time orthopedic surgeon in Coos Bay to $60,000 plus professional pay as a Lieutenant Colonel physician — probably another $20,000 — in Stuttgart. It hit a lot of people hard financially. But we were there to make things better, to do our job and go home."

Bert and Comer told the general about the challenges they'd had since their initial deployment, and how they were treated when they came on active duty — "as second-class citizens," Frosty says.

"The military had a lot of catching up to do," he says. "Our housing and food services were below par when we got there, relative to those on the active duty. But we just dug in and did our job."

Later, McCarthy's chief of staff invited Jeff and Frosty to meet him at his home for lunch. His wife was a skilled dressage rider and took them on a 30-minute ride on their 20-acre compound.

"One might think the wife of a three-star general would be quiet and let her husband rule the roost," Frosty says with a chuckle. "Nope, this lady was in charge. We were sitting in the back of the carriage and her husband was sitting next to her, and if he did something wrong, she let him have it.

"We were treated like royalty, and we were listened to. That was the most impressive thing to me. They wanted to know how could they adapt what we were doing to missions going forward."

Comer found that improvement in medical care because of the Reserves and National Guard was happening "in the States, Europe, the Gulf — everywhere."

"I don't want to sound like this was only us," he says. "But if the active duty medical units wouldn't have had the Reserves and National Guard, they wouldn't have been able to cover their medical needs in the Gulf, Europe or the States. Sixty percent of all medical assets of the military sat in the Reserves and National Guard, since it was too expensive to pay doctors, nurses, pharmacist, etc., to be on active duty.

"This is also why you see so many civilian healthcare workers staffing military hospitals now, many of whom are in the Reserves or National Guard. The lessons learned in the first Gulf War by senior military personnel was that the Reserves and National Guard were an extremely cost-effective force multiplier to the military's ability to complete their mission and that's why you have seen so many deployments over the past 30 years."

After a conflict such as the Gulf War, Frosty says, Congress typically cuts military spending.

"Then we aren't necessarily ready for the next conflict that arises," he says. "That is a mistake. Don't skinny down the military to the point where we won't be ready to protect our country. Government's first duty is to protect its citizens. I have learned from having been on the accordion — draw-down, increase, draw-down, increase. You get pulled and tugged, and your efficiencies aren't consistent."

Comer and the rest of his group were preparing for a long haul that didn't happen.

"It was the most shocking military experience I had, given what we were expecting," Frosty says. "The war was over in about five days.

The medical unit in Stuttgart wound up with "one or two Gulf" casualties.

"We had a few injured soldiers," Frosty says, "and a few dependents who needed treatment."

The move toward home IV therapy had begun, too.

FROSTY'S NO SNOWMAN

"There was a seismic change in the military because of the success I was part of during the Gulf War," Frosty says. "The active-duty military learned — though they didn't implement it right away — that you don't need to keep people in the hospital all the time. You can move them to lower levels of care."

Frosty doesn't regret serving in the Gulf War.

"Having been through Vietnam, and seeing the state of the military health care system, I wanted to help out," he says. "And I learned a lot of things that came in handy later."

Nursing and Administrative staff of the 45th Sation Hospital, Frankfurt, Germany

FROSTY'S NO SNOWMAN

Executive Staff Meeting, 5th General Orthopedic Hospital, Ban Cannstatt, Stuttgart, Germany

CHAPTER 9

HELTER-SKELTER IN HEALTH CARE

Frosty Comer, and most of the 45th Station Hospital, flew from Stuttgart to Fort Lewis, Wash., on March 17, 1991, and was processed from Army active duty back to active Army Reserve status. He came back from the first Gulf War to what amounted to a hero's welcome.

"When soldiers came back from Vietnam, they were vilified, they were spit on, they were called baby-killers," Comer says. "After the fall of Saddam Hussein and the United States kicking Iraq out of Kuwait, we were treated as heroes."

In June, Frosty was among a group of veterans who marched in the Starlight Parade as part of Portland's annual Rose Festival.

"We wore our uniforms and American flags were waving in the crowd as we passed by," he says.

By this time, Frosty was back to work at Vital Choice, which provided home IV therapy and other medications that previously could only be administered in a hospital setting. The patient, family and other caregivers had to be carefully trained (see one, do one, teach one) in order to receive IV therapy in the home. Instead of the hospital taking "total control and liability," the patient and their provider company were responsible for the administration, catheter care and outcome supported by the clinical staff at Vital Choice.

In the short time Frosty had been away, Gary Schnabel, who had been hired to provide pharmacy support while Frosty was overseas, and Frosty's partners had done a great job growing Vital Choice. And suddenly, the competition was flagging.

Option Care, a competitor of Vital Choice, had franchises throughout Oregon and Southwest Washington. Its Vancouver, Wash., franchise was run by Steve Oliva, who owned the Hi School Pharmacy chain. The franchises in Eugene, Medford and Klamath Falls were owned by a physician from Brookings, Ore. The Vancouver Option Care franchise had the OHSU/Care Oregon contract, which was a Medicaid HMO for the whole state.

"But they needed the Option Care franchise in Eugene, Medford and Klamath Falls to cover the southern part of the state," Frosty says.

During that period, California congressman Pete Stark began to look at utilization of healthcare services entities such X-rays, labs and home IV therapy services that were owned by physicians as opposed to those that were not. Stark found the utilization of those services was significantly higher if they were physician-owned.

The result was the "Stark Law." It was a set of federal regulations that prohibit physician self-referral, specifically a referral by a physician of a Medicare or Medicaid patient to an entity for the provision of designated health services, if the physician or a family member has a financial interest with the entity.

That cut into the profits of those franchises such as Option Care, which was owned by a physician.

"As a result, the physician franchise owner out of Brookings wanted to sell their offices in Eugene, Medford (licensed home IV therapy pharmacies with nurses) and Klamath Falls (nursing)," Frosty says.

"They came to us, which was a huge opportunity. "That pulled the rug out from under our Option Care franchise competitor in Vancouver because they could no longer say they could cover all of Oregon. It gave us inroads to the Oregon Health Sciences University (OHSU) contract, which we eventually won along with other Oregon health insurance company contracts. We had copies of all their contracts with other insurance companies like Blue Cross/Blue Shield and Pacific Source. We could cover the state."

Frosty had begun canvassing Oregon looking for potential sites for Vital Choice offices, hitting outposts such as La Grande, Pendleton, Klamath Falls and Medford.

"This acquisition opportunity opened the door for getting us referrals we didn't have before without opening new branches and competing with the established Option Care offices," he says.

In November 1991, Comer drove to Eugene with Dr. Woody English, Vital Choice's medical advisor, to meet with Ken Provencher, the new contracting officer for Pacific Source.

"There was an infectious disease conference being held in Eugene the day before the 1991 Civil War football game," Frosty recalls. "Dr. English and I talked to Ken about the job we do and how we can cover the whole state for all their insured patients and physician providers."

The trio met in the Pacific Source office, directly across the street from the Eugene Country Club.

"The office was decked out in the Ducks' green and yellow," Frosty says. "Ken and I hit it off well. After we finished talking, he said, 'Frosty, I'd like to introduce you to Dr. Bob Loomis, our medical director.' We walked into his office, and I noticed that the carpet was black, the walls were orange and there was every bit of OSU sports memorabilia you can think of in his office."

FROSTY'S NO SNOWMAN

This was right up Frosty's Beaver alley.

"All of a sudden, it hit me how we could get this contract," he says. "My daughter Molly, then a freshman at Oregon State, was a good friend of Jason Barry, a running/blocking back for the Beavers football team."

The next day, Oregon State upset Oregon 14-3 at Autzen Stadium.

"I bought a top-line leather NCAA football, wrote the Civil War game score on it and gave it to Jason, who got all the Beaver players to sign it," Frosty says.

The next week, Frosty had another meeting with Proventure and Loomis. Frosty wrapped up the football and presented it to Loomis as a gift.

"He opened the box and almost started to cry," Frosty says. "He told me, 'You have no idea how much this would cost me at an OSU auction.'

"That next week, the contract was signed."

Selling customers on his business was difficult for Frosty, at least in the beginning.

"I learned I just had to go in and educate people," he says. "In 1991, home IV therapy was still a very new industry. I represented myself as the pharmacist who would be caring for the physician's patient in the home.

We were a hospital in the home. We were administering critical medications that needed to be monitored closely by our nurse, pharmacist and dietician. A lot of people didn't know this could be done, and some of the doctors didn't know about acute care home medicine. We had a huge educational effort to undertake.

"I learned to not be shy to ask the physician to refer patients to us, since we were really good at what we did and had all the licenses and accreditation to provide hospital care in the home. Selling became more teaching, and I got to be very comfortable with that."

Once Vital Choice acquired the assets and assumed the liability of the Option Care franchise in Eugene, Medford and Klamath Falls, the company grew rapidly. Vital Choice didn't own the franchise; it just paid the previous owner for his assets and assumed liabilities.

"Option Care corporate ended up suing us because we still had their computer and software programs we had acquired in those branches," Frosty says. "We did not need them because we had our own."

The case ended with Vital Choice paying $50,000 in an out-of-court settlement and turning over any Option Care manuals, equipment and software.

❄

About this time, Frosty began working with Dr. Mark Loveless, a board-certified infectious disease physician who ran the OHSU HIV/AIDS clinic and later was the state of Oregon's AIDS epidemiologist. Frosty worked with Dr. Loveless to care for his patients with home IV therapy needs and later in the development of new therapies and treatment options.

"For 10 years, I set up the AIDS program at OHSU, did research and a lot of teaching," Loveless says. "During the early days of HIV, we were treating people with infections they got because their immune systems were down. Those treatments required IV therapy. We had to send people home with IVs, because we couldn't keep them in the hospital the entire time.

"Frosty — a pioneer in home IV therapy — was one of the few pharmacists who was willing to take these patients and get them treated. There were a lot of people who didn't want to have anything to do with them."

Loveless and Comer helped develop a plan to work with HIV/AIDs in hospice and Hopewell House.

"That was really important," Loveless says. "As we were starting to see more cases, we were doing essentially end-stage therapy for people who were going to die. We were trying to keep them as comfortable as possible. That is the definition of hospice. The problem with the hospice organizations at the time was they were not prepared for HIV and were not interested in taking care of people living with HIV."

Frosty was a member of the board of directors at Hopewell House.

"We spent a bit of time talking with them, educating them about HIV, reassuring them that HIV wasn't transmitted easily in health care settings, and that they could safely do end-of-life care," Mark says. "Frosty was real important in getting Hopewell House set up in a way that they were willing to take HIV patients. Being a pharmacist, he helped guide some of the medications that were being used in end-of-life care."

Loveless needed Comer's support when there wasn't a lot of it available.

"He always had a real positive attitude about a disease that was difficult and depressing at times," Loveless says. "All of us cared for people living with HIV in those times when we couldn't treat the underlying disease. We had to treat the infections when they came up and care for people as they reached the end of life. That's not a good fit for some."

Loveless says he grew to appreciate Comer for many qualities.

"He is a very generous and creative person, willing to think about how to do things a different way to the patient's benefit," Loveless says. "I always enjoyed working with him because of that. He always thought out of the box. It is a joy to be around somebody like that. Sometimes it was a little challenging because you don't see the same vision. But even the times we differed; the arguments had positive endings. We figured out what we needed to do and got it done.

"Frosty has so much energy. He is a very competitive guy. One of the things that marked him in his business is he was willing to compete with other people doing the same thing. He wanted to be the best. That competitive nature is something I respect a lot. My personality is more collaborative than competitive. We balance each other out. That is why working with him has been such an interesting journey for me. You don't meet many people like that who also have a real strong sense of ethic and a real moral core."

Frosty cites an example of collaborative creativity between himself and Loveless.

"An HIV patient presented with a debilitating case of oral thrush, a fungal infection of the mouth," Frosty says. "The patient's veins were compromised and were not suitable for IV administration of amphotericin, a very potent and difficult-to-administer antifungal."

Comer, with significant ICU pharmacy experience using DMSO in head trauma cases that caused significant brain tissue swelling, suggested to Loveless that he compound an "oral swish and spit, but not swallow" solution of amphotericin in DMSO.

"DMSO is rapidly absorbed through the skin and mucous membranes and can 'carry' other compounds into the affected area," Frosty says. "It turned out to be very effective killing the oral thrush infection and a blessing to the patient, who could now take food and medications orally."

❄

Into 1992, Vital Choice was enjoying success and was looking to expand into the Puget Sound area. The company had started with one branch in Portland and added offices in Eugene, Medford, Klamath Falls and Bend.

"We had grown," Frosty says. "We had some investors asking us to take a look at expanding there. Our Portland branch was able to service patients as far north as Centralia, Wash., but we were looking to add branches in Tacoma and Seattle, and later possibly Spokane and Boise. We had the money to do it."

In 1993, though, the Clinton health care reform plan changed things, Frosty says.

"A lot of companies with private capital that wanted to invest in health care started to dry up," he says. "Was it going to be government-run health care? You don't want to invest in something that you don't know what the outcome will be. The investors started pulling back. We were strapped. You have to have capital to invest.

"We started looking for mergers and acquisitions. Or was it time to sell? We were doing well, but we didn't know what the health care market was going to look like."

The area's hospital systems were gearing up for their own home IV therapy business, too. Though they couldn't service anything outside their immediate geographical area. Health systems like Providence had their own insurance and were not approving of Vital Choice as a competitor provider.

"In addition, Medicare had not yet understood what home IV therapy was," Frosty says. "To this day, it doesn't have an appropriately defined home IV therapy benefit with the industry codes for efficient billing and payment. The Portland Veterans Administration understood it and developed a whole new budget for continuum care, with home health, home hospice, home medical supplies, home IV therapy. They were the first VA in the country that had a home IV therapy contract, and that was with us. It became the 'stem cell' contract for all VA medical centers in the country that later became a very important customer of Coram's Federal Health Services that I started in 2001."

Vital Choice dominated the Oregon/Washington market, with some significant competitors — hospital systems like Legacy and Providence. Vital Choice had a contract with OHSU and had a lot of private insurance contracts. The most important requirement was to get a contract to provide its services with health insurers such as Pacific Care, BCBSO and Health Net. OHSU had a unique relationship with Care Oregon, the Oregon Health Plan HMO (Health Maintenance Organization). Vital Choice had a contract to provide both private insurers and Care Oregon with home IV therapy services.

"We created a company to serve patients, No. 1, with the goal to establish a successful business in the Northwest and expand it, but ultimately to sell the company to an acquirer elsewhere in the country that wanted to have market penetration in the region," says John Castles, the company's executive chairman. "That was our exit strategy. We knew it was an economically viable place for an emerging market, good for patients, and our strategies and planning for the company were borne out in the marketplace.

"We wrote a five-year business plan and hit our five-year numbers in year three. We were in contact with and had knowledge of the national companies in the financial investment marketplace, about what is called a 'rolo,' where companies in that business wanted to expand into the Northwest."

❄

In February 1993, Vital Choice was purchased by Healthinfusion, a national consolidator with its home office in Miami. Vital Choice owners were paid in Healthinfusion stock, worth about $1.2 million.

"And we still had a business," Frosty says. "We were given access to national insurance contracts like AETNA and SIGNA, which a mom-and-pop company like us wouldn't have had otherwise."

Vital Choice moved its office to Tualatin, Oregon.

"When the Stark Amendment took full effect across the country, there was a fire sale of companies," Frosty says. "All of a sudden, these doctors can't do the same business because of conflict of interest in ownership."

In 1994, Coram Health Care was formed.

"I joke that it was formed by the office of the inspector general," Frosty says.

For years, a number of home IV therapy (HIT) companies would approach physicians in a community and get them to invest $30,000 each to form their own HIT (home infusion therapy) company. After a period of time, assuming the physician-owned HIT entity was profitable, T2 Healthcare, for instance, would purchase the company from the physicians in T2 stock.

Everything went well as this model grew throughout the country until Pete Stark started investigating physician-owned enterprises such as labs, X-ray and HIT services and found that there was much higher utilization from those entities that were owned by physicians. The U.S. Office of Inspector General started legal proceedings that forced T2 to sell or dissolve these branches. Several of the companies that had relationships with physicians had to close them down.

In 1994, five large entities formed Coram — T2, Healthinfusion, Medisys, Curaflex Health Services and HMSS. The following year, Coram purchased Caremark Home Infusion to form the largest home IV therapy provider in the U.S.

"It basically cleaned up one part of the industry," Frosty says. "Coram had to have specific language that stated in our contracts that we could not receive any Medicare/Medicaid referrals if there were any physician ownership."

What resulted was an even more chaotic situation, with six different large national companies — a national mega-merger. In Portland, there were only two companies — Frosty's company, which had just become Coram, and Caremark. "Our staffing didn't change much at all," Frosty says. "We incorporated a few folks from Caremark and moved into their office in Durham, OR."

Nationally, things were helter-skelter.

"They were all operating under different business systems," Frosty says. "All the senior and regional managers, and in some cases branch managers and staff, got laid off or had to be incorporated into one functioning unit. You had to decide about what operating systems to use. It was chaos for a couple of years until they finally decided to use the Caremark system.

"Our integration in Portland went significantly smoother than in most cities, since there was the company I started and a Caremark company that supported one of their physician-owned entities. The Seattle Coram merger had nine competing companies that had to merge into one office with only the staffing to support that one office. This resulted in several key people being laid off. They laid off a pharmacy manager whose wife was a nurse case manager at Blue Shield of Washington, which had a million subscribers."

Frosty was asked to repair some relationships but found his own standing in jeopardy. After a merger of companies, Frosty and his two partners were "on the chopping block to get laid off" in Portland.

Says Frosty: "But the senior VP/sales Jim Glynn, who later became the founder of Amerita, another national HIT company, told them, 'You don't want to lay off Frosty, because he has all the relationships with the doctors and hospitals and insurance companies.' So I stayed.

Portland VA Medical Center

CHAPTER 10

CORAM AS END-OF-LIFE FORUM

In the early '90s, there was a budding crisis with American veterans.

"The health of our veterans as a whole wasn't good," Frosty Comer says. "A lot of them were smokers and drinkers. Most were World War II, Korean and Vietnam vets.

"I remember one who had shrapnel in his body that couldn't be removed, and every six months an infection would flare up. The Portland VA would refer him to our home IV therapy services and we would provide him home IV antibiotics for six weeks. Because of hospital-acquired infections, hospitals aren't a good place to be for people with compromised immune systems."

Dr. Tom Ward was the chief of infectious disease at the Portland VA Medical Center. Karen Collell, the Portland VA's infectious disease pharmacist who had worked with me at Good Samaritan Hospital and knew about our home IV therapy services, met with Dr. Ward.

"We need to start getting these patients out of the hospital," Collell told him. "No. 1, our hospitals are full. No. 2, it is not safe to be there and be susceptible to getting more infections."

"But they had no budget for home-care services," Comer says. "The financial incentive then for the VA was to keep people in the hospital. Without a budget to pay us for our services, we created a "barter system" where we would be paid in VA medications that we could use in our normal operations.

"We would take a VA patient home typically on an IV antibiotic and charge our most competitive commercial insurance company's contract prices to the Portland VA. We had to make sure we didn't get any financial advantage because the VA paid about 40 percent less than we did for drugs because of government drug contracts. We got paid with VA drug at the price we would normally pay for it from our commercial wholesaler."

In 1994, the Veterans Administration negotiated with its central office to do a trial Request For Proposal (RFP), which was for two years.

"The home IV therapy trial saved the Portland VA about $100,000 a month for those two years," Frosty says.

By 1996, the Portland VA was given permission to develop a home care services budget that included our services and published for a competitive bid a five-year formal RFP.

"Because of providing our services the previous four years, our willingness to be creative and that we submitted the best pricing proposal, we got the bid," Frosty says.

"The Portland VA Medical Center's RFP became the blueprint for home IV therapy RFPs for any VA in the country. I started getting calls from other Coram employees, for example, from Baltimore. 'Could you help us get a contract?' I would talk to the staff at the specific VA who were responsible for home care services. When the Baltimore officials got a personal recommendation from the Portland VA, they felt comfortable working with us.

"They took the Portland VA RFP, which I helped to write, and replicated it for Baltimore. We submitted a response and won that bid too. I was jazzed."

Frosty began getting invited to display at the annual VA Home Care Conference.

"I was very fortunate, and pleased, to have earned the trust of Mary Jo (Mead)," he says. "We found solutions to their needs and we were not risk-averse. I was always willing to try something. Through my military hospital experiences, I learned how to adapt and create new paradigms."

In 1997, the VA Home Care Conference was held in Crystal City, Virginia. Thanks to Mary Jo, the community health nurse coordinator for Portland VA home IV therapy referrals, Frosty was introduced to the VA nurses at the conference who ran the home programs and presented the concepts of home IV therapy and how it could lead to getting veterans out of hospitals and into home care.

"I was authorized by both the VA and by Coram to provide the opening reception's hors d'oeuvres," Frosty says. "I made sure the hotel that hosted their conference did a great job, which was appreciated by all the VA home care nurses. We became the traditional opening reception sponsor."

Two years later, the conference was in San Antonio.

"Several of the nurses in charge of organizing the conferences asked to take me out as a thank you," Frosty says. "We went to 'Howl at the Moon,' a piano bar on the Riverwalk. It was the first time I had been to this type of venue, and I thoroughly enjoyed the music and company."

The group of a dozen nurses, which included Amy Mitchell and Kay Cash from the Richmond, Va., VA and Donna Vogel from the

Connecticut VA, and Frosty got to the club early and were close to the stage.

"As the crowd continued to grow and a bachelorette group arrived, the two piano players were rocking," he says. "The waitresses were walking around selling long plastic containers of shooters, so several folks had more to drink than they should have.

"All of a sudden, the piano players stopped the music, and someone pulled out a large search light and shined it on me. Everyone was surprised when one of the pianists stood up and said, 'Ladies and Gentlemen, we have a celebrity in the house. Robert Duvall, please stand up.'"

Follically challenged Frosty played along, stood up and waved to the crowd as he was given a loud ovation, as Robert Duvall.

"A couple of the ladies from the bachelorette party, who were in no condition to drive, came over and asked for my autograph on parts of their body," Frosty says with a laugh. "I had to be discreet, but I did accommodate them and then sat down and continued to enjoy the music."

Every year, from St. Louis to Nashville to San Diego to Washington D.C., and New Orleans, Frosty was invited to take part and help with the convention's festivities.

"They had accepted me into their culture as a partner in providing care to our veterans," he says. "I wasn't a slime-ball sales rep who was trying to sell them something they didn't need. It is important to establish credibility for you and your company with your products or services when you are dealing with medical sales of any kind."

After his success with the home care national conferences, Comer was tasked with helping employees from other Coram branches to learn how to work with military and VA healthcare customers.

"I spent half my time teaching the Coram employees how to speak the VA and DoD language he says. "I even had a power point presentation with six slides with about 30 acronyms on each slide that they had to learn."

The chaos at Coram continued into the 21st century. Frosty Comer was working in sales and marketing to physicians and insurance groups, and also served as a backup pharmacist. He was frequently sent to Seattle to help with smoothing over Coram issues with insurance companies.

"Our only big competitors at the time were the hospital systems," Comer says. "They had to give patients, going home from the hospital on IV medications, a choice on what company they could use. We were somewhat restricted in going in the hospitals to market to discharge planners and patients because of HIPAA.

"Being in a bigger company gave us some strategic advantages, though, because we had contracts with the national insurance companies. The insurance company nurse case managers would refer patients to us, which gave us the opportunity to market to hospitals and doctors."

Through the late '90s, Coram's mega-merger integration remained a struggle, but Frosty made it work.

"Because the Portland Veterans Administration was one of my branch's best contracts, the people in other Coram branches and our corporate office started hearing about the VA and Frosty," he says.

Collell and Mead talked Frosty into displaying at a national VA Home Care Conference in Crystal City, Va., in 1997. He staged an opening conference reception at the local Marriott and laid out a nice buffet spread. "I was in sales-education mode," he says. "I helped our company get a contract with the Baltimore VA. Mary Jo was so thrilled. It gave the Portland VA national recognition. They made it happen, but

Karen and Mary Jo were the people who 'lit the fuse' that started the VA trend to create a continuum of care outside of the VA hospitals."

For the next 10 years, Frosty was a fixture at the national conferences.

"I would help them get other exhibitors, and we would pay into a VA Fund to offset the cost of the conference," he says.

The first four years, Coram sponsored the reception.

"It became popular," Frosty says, "and Mary Jo and her team from the Portland VA became renowned as trail blazers in the development of a continuum care program."

Part of Frosty's job as Coram's national vice president of Coram's Federal Health Services during this period was to travel throughout the country.

"I visited 25 to 30 percent of all VAs and military hospitals," he says. "Each VA medical center is so different throughout the VA health care system."

Frosty was also working with Dr. Tom Edes and Dan Schoeps of the VA central office to develop a national VA approach to home IV therapy. In 1999, Ron Jenkins of the National Acquisition Center (NAC) contacted him with a request for a primer on home IV therapy. Edes, Schoeps and Jenkins were tasked separately to write a request for proposal (RFP) for the national office. "They all knew each other," he says, "but didn't know that each of them were working on the same project."

In the end, Jenkins issued the RFP.

"They had no idea if one company could cover the whole country, or if they would need to have contracts with multiple companies," Frosty says. "It was more of a credentialing request for proposal to see who was equipped to provide this 'hospital in the home' service."

The RFP required two VA regions — Veteran Integrated Service Networks,11 and 12 — to be "carved out" for home IV therapy for veteran-owned, minority- or woman-owned businesses, as dictated by the Veterans Affairs Department's contracting requirements.

"There was a nice African American woman pharmacist who owned a pharmacy in downtown Chicago," Frosty recalls. "She had an IV laminar flow hood in her pharmacy but no idea how to provide IV home therapy to two large VA regions. She wanted to subcontract with Coram, where we would provide services, then bill through her and she would get a cut of the business. It was just not possible for us to do that."

When it came time, Mead of the Portland VA was one of six people to fly to Hines, Ill., to evaluate the RFP responses. The Friday before she and the other evaluators were to fly to Chicago, they were told to stand down. A doctor in the VA central office in Washington, D.C., objected to the program.

"He wasn't consulted, didn't believe in it and didn't want it done," Frosty says. "It was s**t-canned by this doctor who probably hadn't experienced home IV therapy and wanted care only provided within the 'walls of the VA.'

"That pissed off a lot of VA people who had been working very hard to develop a more robust continuum of care so veterans could receive care in the home. We had changed the paradigm of the VA and Department of Defense health care system from a bricks-and-mortar system to a robust continuum care that combined home health, hospice, medical equipment and home IV therapy with lower costs and dramatically improved outcomes."

FROSTY'S NO SNOWMAN

The Veterans Administration was starting to invest in tele-health and tele-medicine. Donna Vogel, a nurse at the Connecticut VA, was one of the nurses leading the effort conducting a trial in tele-medicine. Other key figures included Dr. Edes and Schoeps in the VA central office in Washington, DC.

"When Coram would have their quarterly regional and annual national meetings, word got out that I had helped get a contract with the Baltimore VA, people started getting interested," Frosty says.

Frosty was asked to visit the Seattle VA to meet with Frank Yunker, its chief of pharmacy, to present the benefits of home IV therapy.

"It turned out to be one of the more disappointing encountered with a pharmacy manager I had in my pharmacy career," Frosty says. "I figured it would be a semi-slam dunk, but it turned out not be."

Frosty had retired from the military as a pharmacy officer with the rank of full Colonel.

"But I was very respectful when I went to a VA or military hospital not to push my rank or status around," he says. "My tack was, 'I want to help. Let me know if this is a fit for you.'"

Yunker — who was to become the regional pharmacy manager for the Veterans Integrated Service Network No. 20— was certain it was a bad fit.

"I don't believe in what the Portland VA is doing," Yunker told Frosty. "It is a waste of money because my VA drug costs are cheaper than what you would charge me. We have an infusion clinic here that is staffed by pharmacists and nurses, and veterans come in daily to get their IV therapy."

Frosty: "What if they need more than one dose a day? With home IV therapy they can do it at home. What if the catheter breaks or leaks, or the IV pump doesn't work?"

Yunker: "They can go to the emergency room and get it taken care of."

"He said in no uncertain terms he was not interested and didn't need to talk to me anymore," Frosty recalls. "He was not very pleasant about it."

And Yunker wasn't about to put the brakes on his gravy train.

"They were making all their patients come in every day," Frosty says. "They had pharmacists, nurses and technicians on staff in their hospital-based infusion clinic. Instead, he could have contracted for the care in the patients' home. By keeping everything in the hospital, under his control, it gave him a bigger budget, much to the detriment of the veterans.

"He was so focused on his cost of drug versus ours, he didn't consider all the other expenses he had in labor, supplies, equipment and clinic space, which could have been used for another VA purpose. When a true cost accounting is done, it paints a totally different picture, especially when you factor in the cost to the veteran for time, travel and convenience."

In his travels throughout the country, Frosty found other VA officials doing things that were not in the best interest of veterans, especially those that had to travel a distance to receive care at their VA hospital.

"In Tampa Bay, the chief of pharmacy had a relative working in a pharmacy, so there was some nepotism involved," he says. "Did that mean they didn't provide good service? I can't say that. But Coram could not break into that market. And I can say, nepotism was widely known to be a problem with the VA, as well as the politics of VA and military base realignment and closures efforts by the government."

At the Dallas VA, the physician in charge of their home care programs would not use a home IV therapy provider because of the drug costs. One of the Dallas VA veterans, who needed a bi-weekly infused medication to help him breathe, was also in need of continuous oxygen.

The veteran lived over an hour from the Dallas VA but his portable oxygen tank had only 60 minutes of oxygen for his trip.

"Each trip left him worrying if his oxygen would run out before he got to the hospital or home," Frosty says. "This is not the care our veterans deserve."

※

Frosty would periodically travel to Seattle to meet with Larry Searle, an assistant director of pharmacy at the Seattle VA Medical Center. Larry would leave his Seattle VA pharmacy position because of his conflicts with Yunker and became the administrator of the Puget Sound VA Spinal Cord Injury Specialty Unit at the Seattle VA.

Larry and Frosty had first met while in active Army Reserves — Searle with the 50th General Hospital out of Seattle, Frosty with the 45th Station Hospital in Vancouver. Once a month while in the Reserves, their units would travel to Madigan Army Medical Center in Fort Lewis and work together for a weekend as active reservists.

As pharmacy officers, they would talk over lunch.

"I would get whatever information I could about opportunities to expand our home IV therapy services to the Puget Sound VAMC," Frosty says. "It turned out that they eventually did need support for Total Parenteral Nutrition (TPN), where the patient is fed intravenously."

TPN, as Frosty explains, is a very complex compounding process that is prepared in a laminar flow hood in a sterile environment. It is infused daily by the patient after being trained by a Coram nurse, pharmacist and dietitian.

"People can live on TPN without having to use their gut," he says. "There were two companies that bid for this contract. We ended up winning the contract to compound and deliver the TPN to the patients' home, with the clinical management, equipment and supplies coming from the Seattle VA."

Puget Sound VA nurses and pharmacy officials still wanted to manage the lab results and the patients clinically.

"We were just a provider for the TPN and they would send us the orders and coordinate any formulation changes with our clinical and compounding staff," Frosty says. "We would adjust any compounding that had to be done."

It was a breakthrough for the Puget Sound VA to contract out this specific IV therapy service need, because it was more complex than providing IV antibiotics in their infusion clinic.

Frosty recalls a favorite story about a retired Army sergeant who lived in Portland area in the early 1990s.

"Because of radiation treatment for his testicular cancer, he lost a major portion of his stomach and intestinal tract and could not meet his daily nutritional needs orally," he says. "We had to feed him intravenously with a two-liter TPN bag each night while he was sleeping."

The man loved to go fishing and hunting by himself in the Cascades. He had a camper with a generator to power his refrigerator.

"We would make up 14 two-liter TPN bags with vitamins and electrolytes to be added at the time of infusion, and he would hook one up in his camper each night," Frosty says. "He had an IV pump that would administer the TPN over an eight-hour period while he was sleeping. This was how much technology had improved in 20 years and his ability to learn how to manage his own IV therapy."

One night, with everything hooked up in his camper and ready to go, the man's pump failed. He didn't want to lose his camp site, so he hopped in his truck, hung the bag on his gun rack and drove to Bend's St. Charles Hospital, where he talked officials into swapping out his pump.

"He went back to the campsite and spent the next week on his own," Frosty says. "When it came time for him to go home, he took the pump back to the hospital. He brought the old one that was not working back to us for repair. You talk about being independent — 30 years earlier, he would have had to live in the hospital to receive this therapy."

Frosty says the VA and Department of Defense (DOD) have two major conflicts of interest.

"One, they have a use-it-or-lose-it budget," he says. "I had this happen to me at Madigan Army Medical Center in 1973. During Vietnam, we were always having budget challenges. But at the end of each fiscal year, we would be told we have a surplus of money, and in one year, it was a quarter of a million dollars. It was 'use it or you would lose it.'

"So we bought drugs that we didn't need at the time, but knew we would use in the future. Wouldn't you think the taxpayers would like to have the money back? You would never run your civilian business that way."

The other issue, Frosty says, "is even more evil — a 'make-or-buy conflict.'"

"I ran into this at the Seattle VA Medical Center," he says. "If I am the chief of pharmacy and was given $1 million for our department budget, I have that to spend for staff, equipment, supplies and services I am charged to provide. I can hire people, buy product and have it all come from within the VA.

"But what if a veteran lives 100 or more miles away and in the wintertime can't get over the Snoqualmie Pass? How am I going to take care of that veteran? I may have to contract with a local pharmacy to provide their needed services, at least initially."

This would take money out of a VA pharmacy director's control and the VA's contracting department would contract and pay for non-VA pharmacy services.

Making veterans travel to the Seattle VA each day to receive their IV therapy just to be serviced by VA pharmacy and nursing staff, is not in their best interest," Frosty says. "In addition, if there were a complication at home, the veteran would need to come to the Seattle VA emergency room to get whatever problem needed resolution, rather than having a home IV therapy nurse go to the veterans home to resolve the problem."

National VA administrators had to find a way to take care of the rural and mobile patient population of the VA in a cost-effective way. They started looking at building new VA hospitals — billion-dollar hospitals which didn't make financial sense— and to get the care to the veteran in the rural areas so they could at least get the patient an appointment within 30 days. Over a period of about 10 years through the late 1990s and early 2000s, more than 1,000 community-based out-patient clinics — such as urgent care — were built.

"They started pushing veterans to receive their care to communities where the veterans lived," Frosty says. "The VA was mandated to provide care to veterans to within specific mileage and time standards within each VA Medical Center service area.

The VA had a challenge — how to improve their care and to take care of vets spread all over the country.

Now Congress has added a civilian provider network system to the VA, very similar to DOD's TRICARE civilian provider network. Optum has been contracted by the VA to serve essentially the eastern U.S. and TriWest Healthcare Alliance the western part of the country.

"This gives veterans many more choices; a VA Medical Center, a community-based VA Outpatient Clinic or the Optum/TriWest civilian provider network.," Frosty says. "This is far better than many years ago, but the VA still faces significant challenges."

❄

The Hemlock Society was behind the nation's first physician-aided dying legislation. There was an organization called "The Oregon Right to Die," headed by Barbara Combs Lee, that gathered enough signatures to get an initiative on the 1994 ballot that passed the first time, 51 to 49 percent. Oregon was the first state to implement such a law. Enacted in 1997, it allowed terminally ill residents to obtain and use prescription medications from their physicians for self-administration to end their life.

"The Oregon Legislature, afraid we would become a 'death state,' arranged another ballot measure to repeal the Death with Dignity act in 1997, which failed 60 to 40 percent, so the original Death with Dignity law remained," Frosty says.

Legal fights continued through the next decade, including a 6-3 U.S. Supreme Court ruling upholding the right for physician aid in dying in 2006. Since then, Death with Dignity has been a stable, unchallenged part of Oregon statutes.

With his history with home IV therapy and hospice, including helping sister Kim with her late-life care before succumbing to cancer in 1981, Frosty was called upon to help. In 1997, he was asked by representatives of the Portland hospice community to attend a committee meeting of the Hemlock Society in Ann Arbor, Mich. A protest group of between 25 and 50 people, several in wheelchairs or crutches, demonstrated outside the hotel where the meeting occurred.

"They thought if a law were passed to legalize end-of-life treatment, the insurance companies were going to mandate that they kill themselves," Frosty says. The group called themselves "Not Dead Yet."

"Members felt if physician-assisted suicide were legalized, it would put pressure on handicapped people to end their lives to save money," he says. "They were on the alpha side against Jack Kevorkian, who was on the omega side."

The conference lasted two days and was not obstructed by the demonstrators.

"The issue comes down to how do we as a health care provider community not abandon patients at the end of their lives," Frosty says.

Frosty arrived in Ann Arbor carrying a patient-controlled analgesia (PCA) pump in his suitcase. The pump, worn on a belt or in a fanny pack under a shoulder sling, could be programmed to deliver to a patient 100 milliliters of morphine at the strength of 10 milligrams per milliliter.

"You can program the pump, for example, to infuse four milligrams of morphine an hour with a bonus dose of one milligram," he says. "The patient can push a button to administer a bolus dose every 15 minutes if needed for breakthrough pain."

Attending the Ann Arbor meeting were about 30 people, including doctors and nurses from schools such as Harvard, Cornell, Michigan, Ohio State, Washington and Cal Berkeley. Frosty was the only pharmacist there.

"I made sure I was the very last one to be introduced," he says. "When introductions got to me, I said, 'You might think we are from the sticks in Oregon, but we are taking better care of end-of-life patients than anybody in the country, because of the passage of the death-with-dignity act.' "

Nobody there had seen or knew what a PCA pump was.

"I was shocked, since these were Ivy League academics who should have known," Frosty says. "They were providing critical care at end of life and advising patients of their options.

"Their focus had been on ending a life, not providing as much quality life as the patient could have before death. My credibility in that meeting jumped ten-fold when I described what the PCA pump was, how it worked and how we care for terminally ill patients. This was not only in pain management but symptoms as well — vomiting, nerve pain and so on. "

Frosty told the story of sister Kim.

"She was 27, a nurse, and wanted to enjoy as much of a quality life as possible," Frosty told the audience. "Did I want to jump to the final exit? No. My sister Casey, also a nurse, and I provided her total parenteral nutrition and pain and symptom management. We were able to have four months of quality life with her that set the standard for hospice in Oregon."

Frosty then told the story about a patient referred to him for pain and symptom management by Dr. Nancy Crumpacker, an oncologist in Tualatin. The patient had terminal intestinal cancer and was being treated by the Washington County Hospice Association and the Providence home IV therapy service. Crumpacker wanted to order an IV infusion of a drug called Thiopental, a fast-acting barbiturate in the class of an anesthetic.

"It is a rapid-acting barbiturate drug that used to be used as an anesthetic," Frosty told the group. "This patient had been on 1,500 milligrams of morphine an hour and it wasn't touching his pain.

"The Providence home IV therapy and the Washington County Hospice program, however, wouldn't support the patient receiving Crumpacker's order for Thiopental because they thought it would be used to quickly end the patient's life."

Frosty had to get permission from the Coram VP of clinical services, David McCormack, in Florida to prepare the medication. He got the approval and made up a syringe of 60 milligrams of Thiopental for an initial dose.

"The patient had immediate pain relief from the administration of the initial syringe of 60 milligrams," Frosty said. "I also made a liter bag of Thiopental for IV infusion that Nancy set up to run at a steady rate of 60 mg an hour.

"The patient went to sleep with the initial bolus dose and had no pain. He woke up the next morning while still receiving the continuous infusion, and his family had a chance to visit him and to say their goodbyes."

He died later that night of cancer, but not from the Thiopental.

"He was in no pain when he died," Frosty says. "This is what we call 'palliative sedation.' You are putting somebody to sleep, rest or in position to comfortably communicate with the family without being in pain or ending his or her life."

Representatives of the Hemlock group asked Frosty and the other attendees to write an article about palliative sedation at the end of life.

"We wrote a great article on palliative sedation, but it never got published at the time," Frosty says. "The medical journals were afraid to publish it because the implication in their mind was palliative sedation was a means to kill people. It eventually got distributed all over the country."

Frosty was credited as one of the authors of the article along with professors from Harvard, Cornell, Princeton, Washington and Cal Davis.

"That was pretty cool," he says.

FROSTY'S NO SNOWMAN

❄

During this period, Comer was secretary of the Oregon Health Forum. The group held a monthly breakfast meeting at Multnomah Athletic Club on health care topics that would have 100 to 400 people take part. At one meeting, the topic was measures 16 and 51 and end-of-life care.

"The place was packed," Frosty says. "A number of people were dead set against Measure 16. After a couple of cases came to light where we were able to prove a better way of taking care of end-of-life patients was through palliative sedation or patient-controlled analgesia, the Providence Health Care system changed its policy on palliative sedation. The patient was allowed to use it as long as the intent was not to end his or her life."

This allowed for a higher quality of end-of-life care until it came time for the patient to make a final decision on the time and place to die, or to have the disease take them.

"The Clinton administration had advocated for physician aid-in-dying in front of the Supreme Court, but it boiled down to states' rights," Frosty says. "This got the attention of the Catholic health system."

At a national meeting of Catholic bishops, they approved palliative sedation for hospice patients as long as the intent was to control pain and symptoms and not to end life.

"That provided a cultural change in health care throughout the country," Frosty says. "It allowed the Providence hospice program to become a better steward of patients at the end of their life."

Today in Oregon, every hospital is required to have a "compassionate-care team" and to measure and document the patient's pain level on a scale of 0 to 10.

During the late '90s, as the physician aid-in-dying laws were passed in Oregon, policies and procedures were developed. Frosty was a member of an Oregon Board of Pharmacy task force charged with developing policies for pharmacists who didn't want to participate, and for those who did.

"A whole new focus came about on treating the pain and symptoms of patients dealing with end-of-life diseases," says Frosty, who was also on an Oregon Legislative task force formed to develop better care models for patients dealing with pain and symptoms.

There were about 30 professionals appointed to the Oregon Legislative task force — physicians, nurses, pharmacists, naturopaths, clergy, chiropractors, lawyers, insurance people and others who traveled to multiple cities in Oregon for two years to take testimony.

"Two camps evolved from that task force — the hospice camp and the chronic pain camp," Frosty says. "There was an attorney task force member who had fibromyalgia, a difficult condition to treat.

"She was getting very tired toward the end of a long day of testimony. She blurted out, 'I wish we had a hospice for chronic pain.' The light went on with everybody. That was a great idea."

A subcommittee developed a proposal for the Oregon Legislature. It included a pharmacist, nurse and a physician with specialty in pain and symptoms management that would be the consulting clinical service for any chronic pain patient and his or her primary care provider.

"This specialty team would work with the patient's primary care provider to ensure that all pain and symptom treatments were available to mitigate any drug-seeking behaviors and provide a better quality of life," Frosty says.

The proposal was presented to the Oregon Legislature to fund a two-year study to confirm that a better health outcome was possible using this model — one in rural Oregon and one in the Portland area using the respective Oregon Medicaid HMO organizations. The legislators turned it down.

"They decided to fund a "1-800-I-got-pain" number that would be staffed by a nurse providing resources to those patients looking for pain or symptom relief, both for hospice and chronic pain," Frosty says. "It died a year or two later."

※

At Coram's Portland home IV therapy branch, a resource network office was staffed by nurse Misty Taylor. She coordinated the requested care for contracts Coram had with OHSU/Care Oregon and QualMed, which was later purchased by HealthNet.

"These contracts were great from a perspective of service, management and quality," Frosty says.

The services Taylor would coordinate for patients referred to her, were Coram's home IV therapy, as well as services from contractors for home health, hospice, home medical equipment and orthotics and prosthetics.

Coram's CEO, Rick Smith, signed a capitated resource network contract with Aetna for eight eastern states. It was calculated from Aetna's home care services utilization numbers with "no-risk corridors" that could adjust the per-member-per-month payments on a quarterly basis.

"Aetna had great incentive to move as many patients to home care as possible," Frosty says. "When the utilization was significantly higher than Aetna had given Coram, and Coram had accepted, the revenue paid by Aetna to Coram was insufficient to cover the cost of the contracted services that the resource network managed."

Above: 5th General Orthopedic Hospital, Bad Cannstatt, Stuttgart, Germany, 1990.

Left: Dr. Jeff Bert, MD, Chief of Orthopedics, 5th General Hosital, Bad Cannstatt, Stuttgart, Germany, 1990.

Right: General James McCarthy, Deputy NATO Commander & USAEUR Commander & Frosty at Patch Barracks, Stuttgart, Germany, 1991.

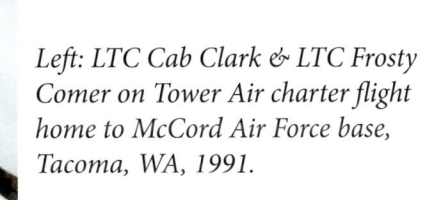

Left: LTC Cab Clark & LTC Frosty Comer on Tower Air charter flight home to McCord Air Force base, Tacoma, WA, 1991.

Above: Jack Aenchbacher, Frosty, Mike Kelly, Tommy Mayes & Kristi Brennan, Coram Federal Health Services Team, at a TRICARE Conference, 2009.

Above: Vicki & Frosty's 25th Anniversary & post-cardiac bypass surgery, Jamaica, 1993.

Colonel Frosty Comer, Army retirement, 1995.

Sandy Willis, Robert Simpson, Ruth Haubner & Frosty, Coram's Federal Health Services Team, at a VA Conference, 2004.

Left: Justin Harmer, Frosty & Brian Zacher at a Joint Forces Pharmacy Seminar, 2007.

Below: Frosty, Cab Clark, Justin Harmer & Evan Romrell at a Joint Forces Pharmacy Seminar, 2009.

Bill Pigeon, Frosty & Ken Huff roommates & classmates at an OSU College of Pharmacy reunion, 2015.

Above: Jim & Barb Ramsey, Mike & Jacquelyn Kelly with Frosty & Vicki at the Alamo Bowl, San Antonio, 2012.

Shauna & Brian Cook at a Cook Solutions Group Company picnic.

Carter, Wendy, Tracy & Randy Neu prepare for a Cook Solutions Group Slingball tournament, 2023

Cook Solutions group sponsored Slingball tournament for Multiple Sclerosis at Pacific City, OR, 2023.

Frosty, Jim Patterson, Rick Sahli & Jack Ward lining up a put 2018

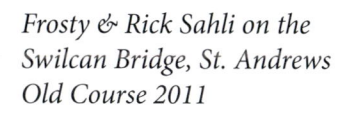

Frosty & Rick Sahli on the Swilcan Bridge, St. Andrews Old Course 2011

Wendy, Vicki, Molly, Brian & Frosty at a Cook Solutions Group annual banquet.

Brian, Wendy, Vicki & Molly

...an Cook, CEO, Cook Solutions Group, ...3.

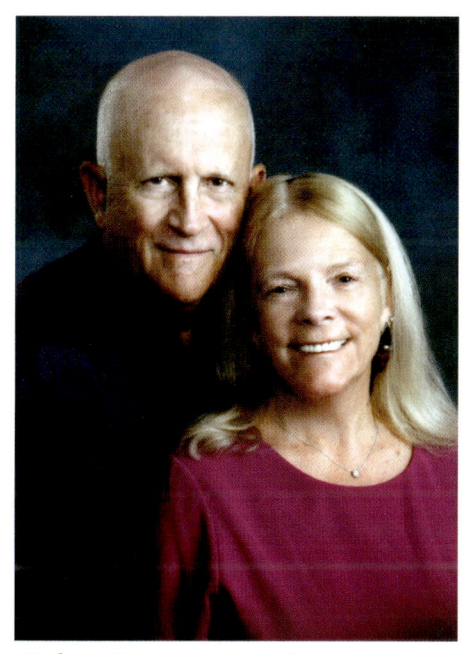

Vicki & Frosty Comer, 2021.

...ook Solutions Group company headquarters, Portland, OR, 2023.

Oregon State University
College of Pharmacy

All profits and donations from the sale of this book will go to the Oregon State University Foundation for the
COMER FAMILY SCHOLARSHIP
in the support of pharmacy students who are in or have been in the military.

https://give.fororegonstate.org/PL1Uv3Fkug

1) visit fororegonstate.org
2) Click Give Online Now
3) Type Comer in the I want to Give to field.
4) Click on Comer Family Scholarship and make your donation

Several resource network-contracted providers, including Apria, sued Coram for lack of payment; Coram then sued Aetna.

"The problem was Coram had no case to sue, since Smith had signed the contract without the ability to adjust to increase home services utilization," Frosty says.

In 1999, Coram went into Chapter 11 bankruptcy to reorganize its organizational structure and operations. Smith was fired, along with several senior managers.

"What was sad," Frosty says, "was the resource network concept and execution was a great tool for the insurance companies, patients and Coram."

Federal Health Services

CORAM
specialty infusion services

Your TRICARE and VA Home Infusion Therapy Provider
CASE*Direct* 800.423.1411 • www.coramhc.com

CHAPTER 11

Cultivating Coram

In 2001, Debbie Meyer took a senior vice president position to run domestic sales for Coram. She became Frosty Comer's boss, a position she would hold for about five years. That same year, Coram hired Dan Crowley as its president, CEO and chairman of the board to navigate Coram out of it's Chapter 11 bankruptcy challenges. Crowley had been president of HealthNet Insurance, which had a subsidiary called HealthNet Federal Services.

"In the early 1990s, his was the only insurance company in the U.S. that bid on a Department of Defense (DOD) contract to change the health insurance component of the military's health care program, called CHAMPUS (Civilian Health and Medical Program of the Uniformed Services)," Frosty says. CHAMPUS became TRICARE in 1993. The CHAMPUS Reform Initiative trial contract was only conducted in California and Hawaii.

Crowley had developed a civilian provider network of doctors and hospitals that were in HealthNet's provider network.

"He had to figure out how to contract with them, how to provide service to military members, their families and retirees and their families and how to have them bill and pay the providers for their service,"

Frosty says. "It was a brand new two-state military DOD initiative. After the first Gulf War build-up, the DOD knew it did not have the medical assets to care for all the military dependents, active-duty personnel and the retirees and their families, totaling 9.6 million members."

After the challenging but successful two-year trial in Hawaii and California, the TRICARE program was expanded to 12 regions throughout the country. It was managed by seven prime contractors with TRICARE Management Activity (TMA), in Aurora, Colo., acting as the manager that oversaw the TRICARE Prime Contractors. HealthNet had a large civilian insurance program but was also the TMA prime contractor for the western U.S. for TRICARE regions 6, 9, 10, 11 and 12.

"They developed a more robust civilian health care network to take care of those who weren't stationed near a military hospital," Frosty says.

Because of all the home IV therapy company mergers and acquisitions that had resulted in the mid '90s, and some poor decisions by senior managers, Coram ended up in bankruptcy starting in 1999. Under Chapter 11, the company was still allowed to operate but had to report to a bankruptcy judge everything that was in its contracts with any type of medical group to make sure it didn't violate the new Stark law.

"Dan was now president of this $350 million company in Chapter 11," Frosty says. "His job was to get it back on track. We had merged six national companies that were working with four different operating systems with hundreds of employees -- a recipe for failure. It took us a long time to determine which of the four systems to use."

Through the '90s, Frosty had been working only with the VA, primarily because there weren't any military facilities in Oregon and the state didn't have a lot of retirees or a robust TRICARE civilian provider network.

"That was just being developed," he says. "However, in the late 1990s and early 2000s, the Portland and Seattle offices started getting referrals for military beneficiaries for home IV therapy out of the Health Net Federal Service's (HNFS) Tacoma office."

Frosty was sent to Tacoma to meet with HNFS nurse case managers, contracts staff and the vice president of the region, Larry Naehr.

"They were accepting of me to develop policies and procedures for how to provide care for home IV services with the nurse case managers and their business office," he says.

Frosty had spoken to Coram officials about the need to develop a focused division in the company that works with just the VA and the DOD.

"There were about 15 million beneficiaries who needed home IV care between the Department of Defense and the VA," he says. "They hadn't done anything up until about 2000 with home care services. Home infusion therapy was a key component to care capabilities for civilian insurance companies, so people could get out of the hospital and receive acute care in the home at a much lower cost with better outcomes."

Coram held a national sales operation meeting in Las Vegas on Aug. 3, 2001 — about four weeks before the 9/11 disaster. Meyer asked Comer to put together a proposal to create a division called Coram Federal Health Services, which was to focus on bringing home IV therapy services to the VA and DOD.

"That's when I had the opportunity to listen to his vision," Meyer says. "Frosty has always been passionate about the military and VA. He knows more about military health care than any other human I know."

"I had prepared like crazy, and Debbie had helped me, but my expertise was on the VA side," Frosty says. "Dan came into the board meeting and told some stories about his experience with the CHAMPUS Reform Initiative. Then he said, 'Frosty, you have 12 minutes to show me you can do it.' I had not a big background in TRICARE, but a good background in the VA and had served 27 years in the military's healthcare system as a pharmacy officer."

Frosty's presentation to Crowley and about 15 senior vice presidents to create a Coram Federal Health Services division was a success.

"Dan totally respected Frosty's knowledge and vision of what greater access home infusion could provide for the military," Meyer says. "He went from being a Northwest pharmacist to heading up the Federal Health Services division for Coram Healthcare, which is now called Coram CVS. Crowley also authorized Frosty to bring on two senior retired military medical personnel to assist him in networking with the current active-duty military medical staff and the TRICARE Prime Contractors to ensure they had the proper claims and payment structure for Coram to provide home infusion therapy to the military beneficiaries."

Meyer wound up impressed with Comer's makeup.

"Frosty is very passionate about everything he does," she says. "He is very knowledgeable on a lot of subjects. He was an excellent mentor for people who followed behind him. He was able to make a difference."

❄

Sometime after the meeting, Crowley pulled Frosty aside.

"I know you are going to need some help," Crowley said. "I would like you to get in touch with Jerry Seiter."

Dr. Seiter was a retired two-star general and a cardiothoracic surgeon who had been the commander of Tripler Army Medical Center in Hawaii and Brooke Army Medical Center in San Antonio, two of the military's larger medical centers. Jerry had retired from the military and worked for Health Net Federal services as the TRICARE Region VI administrator in Texas and Oklahoma. Seiter was hired in early 2002 as a consultant for Coram Federal Health Services. He was on the job through 2005.

Frosty also hired retired Colonel Linn Danielski, who like Dr. Seiter was living in San Antonio. Danielski had been the chief of pharmacy, and Frosty his assistant chief at Madigan Army Medical Center in 1972 and '73.

"Linn and I were good friends in the early 70s and stayed in contact for all those years until 2002," Frosty says.

In the late 1990s and early 2000s, TRICARE had 12 regions and seven prime contractors — insurance companies that had developed civilian healthcare networks that had the ability to refer patients to providers, process their claims and pay providers. As Frosty perused the contracts Coram had with all the VAs and TRICARE entities, he noticed something puzzling.

"Every VA medical center facility is its own payer," Frosty says. "I started finding a payer ID names that said 'VA.' I would see someone at Coram, who didn't know the VA system, would stick a branch's claim in this 'VA' contract bucket, but with no indication which VA Medical Center it was."

Something was fishy.

"I discovered there was a Virginia Medicaid claim in the VA payer name because 'VA' was the initials of the state of Virginia," he says with a chuckle. "I had to clean up Coram's contract numbers and names, and I had to make visits to the corporate office of all seven contractors in the country to make sure they had our branches properly loaded with our proper payer numbers and names. It took six months to get everything corrected."

Coram was working with 154 VA facilities throughout the country.

"It became a real challenge to right-size the contracts," Frosty says. "When it came to the military's healthcare system, TRICARE, I had to go to Aurora, Colo., where I met David Bennett, the health care program specialist for reimbursement for TRICARE Management Activity."

Comer says he considered Bennett "a breath of fresh air" in working through a complex government system.

"David was knowledgeable, competent and trusted me after I explained this new way of caring for complex patients in their homes," Frosty says. "David and I developed a close working relationship in which we had mutual trust. By 2004, we developed policies, procedures and codes for services that weren't normally provided in the Medicare benefit.

"To this day, I'm so thankful that I found David Bennett. The work that we did to bring home IV therapy to the military is now embedded in the TRICARE Reimbursement manual. This is the formal recognition of the value of our service and the paradigm change in providing 'hospital care in the home.' "

DOD/TMA administrators realized having 12 regions and seven contractors made things too complicated. Soon they cut the regions to three — Humana Military Health Care Services had the South; Health-Net Federal Services had the North and TriWest Healthcare Alliance had the West.

For awhile, Comer was traveling throughout the country at least three weeks a month.

"We were growing 15 to 20 percent a year," he says. "We were getting closer to getting out of Chapter 11."

In 2004, Frosty was allowed to hire three regional managers to help continue Coram's Federal Health Services growth. The hires: Sandy Willis of Salt Lake City for the West, Ruth Haubner of Columbus, Ohio, for the North, and Robert Simpson of Columbia, S.C., for the South.

Frosty met with the trio in San Antonio in the summer of 2004 to develop strategies for how to work with the VA and the DOD medical treatment facilities. After a few months, Simpson transferred to the Patient Financial Services Department of Coram. Frosty hired Mike Kelly of Boerne, Texas, to handle the South.

Coram was growing fast. Frosty made two more hires — Terri St. John of St. Louis as vice president of the VA and Tommy Mayes of San Antonio as vice president of DOD/TRICARE.

"Tommy was instrumental in helping me change the paradigm of the military and VA health care system to a much more robust continuum of care," Frosty says.

Mayes was a retired Army Lieutenant Colonel who had been a Black Hawk helicopter pilot during the Iraq War and later became a hospital administrator with a Masters degree from Baylor. Frosty hired him in 2005 as VP of Coram Federal Health Services.

"We opened the minds of the TRICARE system to keep people out of the hospital, keeping them at home, when possible," Mayes says. "There was some reluctance on their part. We broke down those walls. TRICARE, the VA and the patients from those health care systems were able to benefit from the effectiveness of home care infusion."

Comer and Mayes worked together for more than six years.

"Frosty is a dynamo," Mayes says. "He has a very high energy level, is very passionate about what he does. He is also a very dedicated patriot who loves this country. I learned a lot from him. He was fun to work with. If I ever needed his advice, I knew I could ask."

Mayes learned something else about his friend.

"We were at a meeting with some administrators, and Frosty was talking, and he wouldn't stop," Mayes says with a chuckle. "We had already sold our idea to this group. Finally, I said, 'Frosty, stop talking. We've made the sell!' He was overselling. When he is in full gear, you are not going to get him to shut up."

❄

With Seiter and Danielski no longer employed by Coram — "they had more than served their purpose and wanted to move on to other things," Frosty says — I was able to hire a military/VA consulting company called Medical Services International."

The company was founded by a couple, Jim and Barb Ramsey, and also worked with a colleague named Roberto Gonzales. Jim had served in the Army in Vietnam, working as a combat medic on a Medevac rescue unit, 1st Cavalry Division. He was shot down three times and wounded, decorated five times for heroism with the Silver Star. After the final shoot-down in 1969,

Ramsey returned to the States in 1969 and met Barb, who was a nurse at a Fort Sill, Okla., hospital.

Within six months, they were married. Today, they have been married 52 years. They both stayed in the military for many years. Jim retired from the Army as a Major; Barb retired as a Colonel. They live in San Antonio.

Once recovered, Jim became lead agent to represent the Army in negotiation with the Air Force and Navy "whenever we decided to mix programs."

"I traveled all over the U.S., flying into hospitals and medical treatment facilities," he says. "With that, I gained a lot of knowledge about the needs and services required to be purchased outside the military system."

The Ramseys met Frosty at a VA hospital conference.

"He was quite the entrepreneur and, as we later learned, a great human being," Barb says. "Through the years, it was fun to watch all the initiatives that he designed and grew into successful businesses."

MSI specialized in introductions to the military and VA.

"We were able to identify projects and helped make connections to get people like Frosty's company (Coram) in front of the decision-makers," Jim says. 'We opened the doors for companies that wanted to work with TRICARE and VA. They would come to me and say, 'We have this product, this service.' Frosty had a home IV therapy solution for both. Coram was coming out of bankruptcy at the time and hired us to make those connections."

Frosty was a connector, Barb says.

"One of the things about the TRICARE and VA is they don't understand incentives on the commercial side," she says. "The VA would not do business with any company that did not have a specified accreditation. Frosty was one of the folks instrumental in getting them to learn that the opportunity and accreditation they were so strict about wasn't the only game in town. It opened opportunities for others."

MSI worked with Coram for eight to nine years.

"We helped them grow from a $12 million company to $300 million," Jim says.

The Ramseys and Frosty and Vicki Comer became friends outside of business.

"There is not a better human on the planet than Frosty," Jim says. "He is the best. He will do anything for you; so will Vicki. He gives so much of himself to the community, to young people."

"They are such giving people, dedicated to military and to helping people," Barb says. "It is amazing to see the depth of their benevolent actions. Frosty fosters that atmosphere where he helps people out and is willing to help build businesses."

"Frosty is short, but he is the most competitive person you will find," Jim says. "At any sort of contest — shooting hoops, throwing footballs, baseball, golf, anything — he is tenacious. He will not quit. If you beat him once, he will want to beat you 100 times."

"Frosty cheats at everything," Barb says. "One time we were at their house, and he had a foosball table in the garage. It is a game I have never acquired any skill at. Vicki was on Frosty's team but was trying to coach me through it, and he got so mad. 'Quit helping her! I'm trying to beat her.' And he was serious."

The Ramseys caught a taste of the Comers' college allegiance when the latter visited San Antonio for the 2012 Alamo Bowl game between Oregon State and Texas.

"They arrived in total Beaver attire," Barb says with a laugh. "They were in orange from head to toe — Beaver hats, shirts, socks. They were quite the colorful characters at the Alamodome."

❄

The Ramseys and Gonzales came in handy to Coram when, in 2005, TRICARE changed its policy for reimbursement of the medication used in home IV therapy service.

"The pricing they were paying us was now under our costs for the medication," Frosty says.

Robert Simpson, then working for the billing and reimbursement team at Coram, discovered the TRICARE pricing change and brought it to Comer's attention.

"Had the Ramseys and Roberto not helped us get to the medical director of TRICARE to change the policy back to the old reimbursement system, we would have had to close up shop and no provider could afford to provide home IV therapy services to our military families," Frosty says. "Our slogan was, 'No margin, no mission.' We were told by many doubters we would never get this changed; we got it changed in four months thanks to Jim, Barb and Roberto. But it took us two years to get $4 million of drug underpayments paid back."

As Coram was coming out of Chapter 11, the judge overseeing its bankruptcy fired Dan Crowley.

"The judge on your case oversees operations and has control and can hold corporate executives accountable for successes or failures," Frosty says.

Crowley had been working as a principal on the Cerberus Capital Management company side and getting paid a venture capital salary as well as making a salary with Coram.

"The judge in the case didn't like that double-dipping," Frosty says. "But Dan did a great job for us."

Bain Company, a management consulting firm, was hired to evaluate operations and make changes to improve efficiencies.

"They cleaned house at Coram," Frosty says. "I lost a vice president, Terri St. John, and a regional manager, Ruth Haubner, even though my division was growing 20 percent a year. I was pissed. And I lost my boss Debbie Meyer. She was clearing the way through the bureaucracy in Coram and helping me get the resources I needed."

John Arlotta, a retired U.S Army Reserve Captain, was brought in to run Coram and make sure the company continued to operate successfully. Arlotta then negotiated the sale of Coram to a company called Apria, the nation's largest home oxygen and respiratory therapy company.

FROSTY'S NO SNOWMAN

"John was a great CEO," Frosty says. "He wanted no excuses; he wanted results. If you had a problem and went to him, you better have a solution too.

Arlotta called a meeting of senior managers in Denver, with several VPs of billing, collections and operations in attendance. The meeting started with Arlotta and Comer sitting side by side.

"Frosty, you either don't know what you are doing, or you are not doing your job," Arlotta said in front of the group. Luckily, Frosty had done pre-meeting research about why the administrators with the Salt Lake City Veterans Administration were complaining they had not been billed for more than six months.

The Coram Sacramento billing center had moved a VA-trained billing technician, who had been responsible for the Salt Lake City VA, to another position and had not notified Coram's FHS team. In addition, the Coram Salt Lake City branch manager had failed to notice his Salt Lake City VA customer had not been billed.

"When I presented the facts to John in front of the other VPs, they started squirming," Frosty says. "A few months later, because of John's leadership, our FHS VA accounts were centralized in Coram's St. Louis billing and collection branch successfully managed by Christine Gregory, Steve Sobel and Brian Briley.

"Within the second month, accounts receivable had dropped by 50 percent and continued until it met the company's standard, or better. All the vice presidents, who had been complaining about our FHS team, were on pins and needles. They didn't mess with me anymore."

There were a number of VPs with egg on their face, and they soon learned that communication and cooperation was better than complaining about something they didn't understand."

❄

In 2007, Coram became an acquisition target and was purchased by Apria. A year later, Apria and Coram were purchased by Blackstone, a firm that "buys companies, improves them and then flips them," Frosty says. The sale price: $350 million.

"For a year, we were a two-headed company with an executive for Coram and an executive for Apria," says Frosty, who served as national VP of Federal Health Services for both entities. "We transitioned all of Coram's oxygen and durable medical equipment (DME) to Apria and they transitioned all their home IV business to Coram."

Management of the Coram and Apria branches had difficulty working together under the corporate ownership of Blackstone.

"I saw an opportunity to create synergy," Frosty says. "A lot of home IV patients needed oxygen or respiratory therapy services. I argued that Apria needed to turn over all its accounts with the VA and TRICARE to our Coram FHS team, since we were already successful, so we could manage them under one umbrella."

Frosty flew to California and met with the Apria administrators.

"They wanted me to bring all the Coram accounts over to Apria," he says. "That didn't make sense. Our Coram FHS program was much more robust than theirs."

In 2008, Dan Greenleaf was hired as CEO/president for Coram, and then assumed the same role with Apria. Greenleaf had been a captain in the Air Force and a navigator during the Gulf War. His father, Abbott, was a three-star Air Force general who had graduated from West Point.

"When Dan found out who I was, what I was doing and that I was a retired Colonel, he understood what that meant," Frosty says. "He became a great supporter and friend."

Greg Meadows became Frosty's direct boss.

"He made sure that Apria's book of business was transferred over to me under Coram's FHS division," Frosty says. "I had responsibility for both Coram and Apria, all VA facility accounts, DOD health care facilities, and TRICARE contracts."

For Apria's FHS team coverage, Comer hired Pam Peck to oversee the North region, Polly Long in the South and Mark Roberson in the West. They were matched up with their respective Coram FHS regional managers -- Kristi Brennan in the North, Mike Kelly in the South and Jack Aenchbacher in the West. They were responsible for working with the VA and DOD customers in those regions for Apria's book of business, and to coordinate sales and service activities with the Coram regional managers of FHS.

"The synergy was successful," Frosty says, "and both Coram and Apria FHS business grew beyond the corporate goals. We had made some great strides in Coram's book of business with the branches in San Antonio and Austin. Coram had contracts with the VAs as well as TRICARE. Apria had contracts with TRICARE, too, but hadn't done much with sales. Coram was able to piggyback with Apria to help the sales pull through."

At 67, travel and the extra work was becoming a challenge for Comer. Coram had created a team that was able to thrive on its own. He decided to retire in May 2011.

"I wanted to spend more time with my grandsons, my daughters and my wife," said Frosty, who stayed on as a consultant with Coram for two additional years. He left the ship in good hands.

"When Debbie Meyer took over in 2001, Coram was grossing $3 million in annual FHS revenue," he says. "By the time I left Coram and Apria in 2011, our FHS team was generating more than $300 million a year in revenue.

"I hate to use money as a measuring stick for health care, but that shows you the paradigm shift for the Department of Defense and VA from a brick-and-mortar (hospital only) health care system to a continuum care that included significant comprehensive home care services."

Since Coram continued to be more successful than Apria, Blackstone decided to sell Coram to CVS Caremark in 2014. When Coram was sold, the price was $2.1 billion.

FROSTY'S NO SNOWMAN

Wendy, Brian & Molly while attending Beaverton High School.

CHAPTER 12

Cook's Recipe for Success

"It is the very people who no one imagines anything of who do the things no one can imagine!"

From the movie "Imitation Game"

Wendy Comer was born on Nov. 2, 1970, in Vicenza, Italy, during their father's first tour in the U.S. Army. Less than 17 months later, on March 31, 1972, Molly Comer came into the world. Their parents, Frosty and Vicki, decided, "Why wait?"

"The doctors were so great at the Army's 45th Field Hospital in Vicenza," Frosty says, "and we had no idea where we would end up, so we figured let's go ahead and have our two kids."

After Frosty's 4 ½ years of active duty, his graduate school and ASHP hospital pharmacy residency during the children's early years, the Comers lived in Beaverton's Highland Hills. In 1985, when Wendy was a high school sophomore and Molly was in eighth grade, the family moved to the Sexton Mountain area.

The Comer girls played sports and were socially active as high schoolers, and their popularity was palpable.

"They were cute and had a lot of friends, and the guys started hanging out with them," Frosty says. "Their friends started coming to our home. Along with our volunteering for school activities and sports coaching, this allowed Vicki and me to get to know many of their friends well."

One of the boys was Brian Cook, who was in Wendy's class in school. Brian had attended Whitford Middle School; Wendy had gone to Highland Park.

"Wendy and I had a class together my first year at Beaverton High," Brian says. "She sat in front of me.

We became pretty tight friends."

"First semester, sophomore year, we first started talking in English class," Wendy says. "We later had Spanish together. He was great — a nice guy."

Brian would become a regular visitor at the Comer home. He developed a special relationship with Frosty and Vicki.

"I loved them," Brian says. "Vicki took me under her wing — I called her 'Mom.' She and Frosty helped me through some challenging times. I loved the family atmosphere and how they raised the girls. I shared their interest in sports. The overall family experience was something I wanted and needed."

Brian grew up the oldest of three children (with brother Craig and sister Christy) to Monte and Donna Cook. Monte was an architect. Today, Brian describes his relationship with his parents as "repaired."

Brian played Little League baseball and youth basketball growing up. He played three years of varsity soccer as a center/midfielder for the Beavers.

"I was into sports," he says. "I wasn't very good at the academics. I didn't study. I didn't apply myself. I just wasn't interested in the academic side of it. I was more into the social scene."

"Brian was hanging out with some kids who weren't focused on school," Frosty says. "When he came to us, he had no passion to excel. He just didn't care. He didn't care if he graduated. He was challenged to graduate from Beaverton High. He was kind of a lost soul."

Brian says there were times when he indulged in alcohol and drugs while in high school.

"Not excessively, but some," he says. "I smoked (cigarettes) from about age 15 to 18. I hated it. I went for a run one day and then lit up a cigarette and I thought, 'This is the dumbest thing in the world.' "

When Brian was 14, his parents divorced. His mother stayed in Beaverton. His father moved to Portland. Did Brian feel abandoned?

"Yeah," he says. "But he never turned his back on me. He was always there for me. It was the right move for him. It wasn't working out with my mom."

It put Brian in a dilemma. In order to stay at Beaverton High — and importantly, to continue to play for the school's soccer team — he had to maintain a Beaverton address. That meant his mother's place, though he wasn't getting along with her. His siblings were there with his mother. At the time, Brian preferred being at his father's. But really, he most liked being at the Comers.

"Brian found our home to be safe, fun and accountable," Frosty says. "We had a family unit. We would sit down and have dinner together. We had rules. The girls were good for him. Our daughters' friends were really good kids, good people to be around.

"He had hung out with some kids who weren't good for him, and despite being very smart, he had no motivation for excelling in school. He was an excellent athlete and a starter on the Beavers' soccer team. This, along with our daughters' help and encouragement, pushed him to complete high school. With Vicki's motherly support, our daughters' friendship and my tough love, he began to flourish."

Brian never did get permission from his parents to "live" with the Comers.

"It didn't matter," he says. "I wasn't talking to my mom, and my dad didn't really care. I was in and out of the Comers' house. From the end of my sophomore year until through my senior year, I lived there and at my dad's house."

Says Wendy: "His Dad and his Dad's girlfriend had a place above Dunaway Park. That's where Brian really lived, but he would stay at our place on and off."

Brian would bring some of his male friends to the Comers'.

"Our house was a place where the kids hung out," Vicki says. "It wasn't always the happiest time for Brian at his mother's. There would be times when I would be sitting on the end of the bed and we had some deep, emotional discussions."

"But I think our home was a happy place for him. Brian would be here on Sunday mornings. We would all have breakfast. He got close to Molly. When he lived here, I did a lot of motherly things for him. Brian needed nurturing, and we nurtured him. I loved having a boy around the house. He would do anything I asked him to do. He was very caring, and he was very family-oriented with us. He went on vacations with us. He was treated like part of our family."

Brian wasn't afraid of work.

"I started working making pizza at Papa Aldo's at 15," he says. "That was a fun job. Later, in high school, I worked as a laborer for a construction company. There were a lot of things, social events, I missed out on because I had to work."

Craig Cook didn't have the problems with their mother that his older brother did. Craig continued to live with her through the end of high school.

"Our relationship was good," he says, "but it wasn't the best of times back then. Brian was carving his path, and I was carving mine. Everything comes with a nasty divorce. Everybody involved … if we could do it over again, I'm sure we would do it a little bit differently.

"I can appreciate where the Comers' heart was at. No doubt they love Brian very much."

Brian's difficulties with his mother took their toll on him.

"It was pretty rough," he says. "The Comers helped out there. I didn't talk to my mom for a good 10 to 15 years. That changed when I got older and wiser. It was in my 40s when we finally started reconnecting."

Being at the Comers, he says, "gave me a sense of family and grounded me a bit."

Frosty and Brian played one-on-one basketball in the Comers' driveway and went at it in foosball. Frosty regards Brian as the son he never had.

"I would agree," Brian says. "I have a deep relationship with my father, but Frosty was a good mentor. He taught me a lot and helped me through those rough times."

Wendy was a foil for pranks by the boys.

"Brian had bought an Oregon lottery ticket with the same numbers that had won the day before," Frosty recalls. "So, we come downstairs for Sunday breakfast, and Wendy is there and is reading the newspaper. Brian says, 'Hey, I bought a lottery ticket yesterday.' He hands it to her and says, 'Can you check out the winning numbers?' She looks at it and her eyes get big. She jumps up and says, 'We won.

We won $20 million!'

"Pretty soon, we told her the truth. We were laughing so hard. 'You bastards,' she said."

"There was a five- to 10-minute window where Wendy thought none of us would be working again," Brian says with a laugh.

Says Wendy: "That was funny/not funny. It still pisses me off. I cannot tell you how mad I was at that. Everybody thinks it was so funny, but it was not funny. I did not pay attention to the dates. We are talking millions of dollars. I went to my room and locked the door."

A short while later, Wendy returned for Christmas after her first term at Oregon State to a surprise.

"I talked to Brian and convinced him to tell Wendy I was going to turn her room, in the Comer house, into a billiards room," Frosty says. "I had purchased a sound system, but I wrapped it up and unscrewed the handle of a push broom to make it look like was a pool cue."

Brian approached Wendy and said, "I'm not supposed to tell you, but … "

"Wendy was in tears thinking I was kicking her out of the house," Frosty says. "Vicki wasn't clued in and was really pissed at me for doing it."

"Actually, Mom was more upset about it than me about that one," Wendy says. "I was like, 'Hey, it was a joke.' That was a bigger joke on Mom."

By that time, Brian had graduated from Beaverton High and was attending Portland Community College. Would he have graduated from high school without the Comers' guidance?

"That's a good question," he says. "I barely graduated, anyway, so probably not. I cared, but I was more focused on the social life than the academics. I put no energy into it."

Brian would go on to do two years at PCC.

"I took so many courses both at PCC and Microsoft classes, I had the equivalent of Microsoft certification," he says. "I didn't get the actual certification, but it opened my eyes on academics. I really got into economics and accounting. ... I started finding myself and actually enjoying my studies."

In the meantime, during the summer after his senior year at Beaverton High, Brian had landed a job at Mosler, a security company specializing in financial institutions.

"At the time, Vicki was in charge of the construction and maintenance of Far West Federal's bank branches throughout Oregon," Frosty says. "One of her vendors was Mosler. The senior manager asked Vicki if Brian would like to work part-time as a casual laborer."

"We used Mosler for ATMs," Vicki says. "Their senior manager, Rich Craig, knew Brian was coming to our house, knew his situation and asked, 'Do you think he would like to be a casual laborer for us?'

"I told Brian he was going to go to work for Mosler. I knew he wouldn't have a problem with that. He did some construction work with his dad, so he was a hands-on person."

Cook wound up working at Mosler for 14 years, at first serving part-time in a warehouse. He worked hard but used a little ruse to inflate his reputation.

"I would move all the stuff from one side to the other side of the building," he says. "The senior manager would come in and say, 'Man this kid is busy.' I was actually doing nothing but moving stuff around to look busy."

Brian worked his way up in the company, first getting hired as an apprentice service technician, then as a fully licensed low-voltage service technician. He wound up being manager of the Oregon/Southwest Washington branch.

"This is where Brian found his passion and calling, starting at the bottom," Frosty says. "He learned the business. His branch was one of the few successful ones in the Mosler system. Brian worked extremely well with the blue-collar employees and was able to negotiate a profitable contract with his financial institution and other customers."

But Mosler had national financial problems, declared bankruptcy, and had to close all its branches in 2000. Brian was immediately hired by another company, Montech Securities, as its Pacific Northwest branch manager.

"The bankruptcy happened on a Thursday," Brian recalls. "I started working at Montech the next Monday. The funny thing is, I brought 15 to 20 of my crew from Mosler. Their biggest complaint had been that they never got any time off. We were working in four days."

Ironically, the Montech office was within walking distance of the offices at Coram, where Frosty was employed. Brian had bought a house and was living in north Portland.

Brian's branches at Montech were successful, but similarly to Mosler, Montech had national financial issues. In 2002, the company was on its way to bankruptcy. Before it happened, Brian resigned.

"I learned a lot of valuable lessons along the way," Brian says, "of what not to do."

❄

Meanwhile, Molly Comer had graduated from Oregon State in business and accounting in 1994.

"I honestly didn't want to go to Oregon State," she says. "I wasn't looking to go there. I went there to play soccer. If I had it to do over again, I probably would have gone somewhere else. I enjoyed my time there, but I didn't like what happened to me in soccer."

School went well, and she joined older sister Wendy at the Kappa Kappa Gamma sorority, making lifetime friends.

Molly had been an all-state soccer player at Beaverton and made the varsity team at OSU as a freshman.

"I lasted a couple of months," she says. "It was only the second year of the program. The coach was completely inept. He got fired, and his successor recruited me to come back. I missed soccer, so my junior year I went back out — and I got cut."

Molly passed her CPA exams and began with Deloitte and Touche in Portland a couple of months after she graduated from OSU. She became a national recruiter and manager of the accounting firm's audit department. Molly was in charge of the audit when Columbia Sportswear prepared its IPO when it became public, and when Kroger bought Fred Meyer — two very large business transactions.

"I loved my job and the people I worked with," Molly says. "It was a great company. I had a great training ground and mentors. But it was corporate America — a lot of work. You would work more than 60 hours a week during busy season, January through April. It is one of those churn-and-burn places. You learn a lot, but people don't typically stay because it is super demanding and a competitive environment."

Molly worked there for 10 years. In 2002, she married Aaron Angelo. They would have three boys — Joey, Tony and Brady.

About that time, Montech was going under.

"I knew Brian wasn't happy there, anyway," Molly says.

FROSTY'S NO SNOWMAN

Small Private Company Honorees
Cook Security adds two more markets

Molly Angelo
Chief financial officer
Cook Security Group

Hometown: Beaverton.

Professional history: I began my professional career in 1994 with Deloitte & Touche. During my nine-year tenure at Deloitte, I earned my CPA certification and received extensive experience in auditing large, public companies in Oregon (Columbia Sportswear and Tektronix were two of my larger clients). In my last promotion at Deloitte I was appointed a senior audit manager and worked in this capacity for about two years before leaving after the birth of my first son in 2003.

I officially began working for Cook Security Group in 2004 as the chief financial officer. When I began as CFO, Cook Security Group had approximately 15 employees and $2.9 million in revenue. During my time as CFO we have grown to $9.6 million in revenue during 2009 and more than 70 employees.

What your organization does: Cook Security Group sells, services and installs all electronic and physical security products and ATM products to financial, commercial and government institutions.

Significant challenges you've faced as a CFO since 2009 started: Making the decision to open branch offices in two new markets (Spokane, Wash., and Reno, Nev.) during one of the most challenging economic times we have seen in the past 70 years.

How you met those challenges: We invested in the right people to lead us in these markets and used our reputation of excellent service at an affordable price to help us gain market share during a time when many companies are looking to strengthen their vendor relationships and get more bang for their buck.

Most significant issue your organization currently faces: In the service and security industry responsiveness and trust is the utmost important element of our business. In order to accomplish this day in and day out we must constantly challenge our employees to elevate their performance to the next level. This takes a team approach across all business centers and departments that must be cultivated by the leadership of the company.

How you relax: I typically use exercise as my form of relaxation. Staying fit and active helps to relieve stress and clear my mind. A nice glass of red wine in the evening or a weekend away at Pacific City with my family are also about as good as it gets.

Charitable or political cause: Before becoming a parent I have always had a passion for our little ones and became involved with youth by joining the board of Young Audiences and the YWCA as well as coaching young girls in soccer for eight years. Currently I am on the finance council for St. Joseph's Catholic church and school and am a volunteer soccer coach for Vancouver United.

Best read from the past 12 months: "Quiet Strength: The Principles, Practices, & Priorities of a Winning Life" by Tony Dungy.

Favorite travel destination: Either Greece or Lake Como, Italy. My husband is Italian and it was a ton of fun to go there and experience the culture with him.

A bit of personal trivia: My six-year-old son Joey is currently my "mentor" in life due to the simple ways he approaches each and every situation.

CHAPTER 13

'NEVER IN OUR WILDEST DREAMS'

With two jobs down the drain in two years, Brian Cook was looking to be his own boss in any new venture.

The 34-year-old Cook knew the security business, so he started building a business plan. And he asked a good friend for help.

Molly Comer was well into a successful accounting career with Deloitte and Touche when Cook came calling.

"Brian came to me and asked, 'Do you want to start a new business?'" Angelo says. "I kind of laughed at him. But we decided to go for it."

"Molly was skeptical because of Brian's lack of a college education," says her father, Frosty Comer, "but he was not to be deterred."

"We spent many hours together," she says. "I had to learn about the business. It is hard to write a plan if you don't know the business."

"We burned the midnight oil coming up with one," Brian says. "We sat up until 3 a.m. one night working on the plan, and when I shared the numbers with her, she laughed and said, 'This is crazy. This isn't going to work.'"

Brian didn't have the capital to qualify for a government Small Business Association (SBA) loan, so he started approaching friends and acquaintances to become investors without any luck.

"I have applied for financial help and everyone said no," Brian told Frosty one day.

"You have to have perseverance, and if you know what you're doing is right and good, you keep plowing ahead," Frosty responded.

"No one imagined anything Brian would do would amount to anything," Frosty says today.

This is all part of Frosty's philosophy in life and business. He points to a saying: "Beware of the soft bigotry of low expectations."

"This applies to a lot of minorities," Frosty says. "All through history, Irish, Mexicans, African Americans and other minorities in their time, have been told they're not worthy and will fail. Equity doesn't guarantee equal outcomes, but you can guarantee equal opportunity. In order for people to succeed, you must provide them with the basic education and opportunities. Equality is a much better word than equity. Equity implies equal outcome. It's up to the individuals to create their outcome."

At first, Cook and Angelo figured about $20,000 in capital would be required to acquire an SBA loan of between $150,000 and $200,000, enough to start what would become Cook Security Group.

"I signed my life away — my house, my car, my lawnmower — every asset I had," Brian says. "I didn't have a lot of equity. Getting a loan with no collateral was pretty challenging."

Was he nervous about the situation?

"Oh yeah," he says. "After I quit my job, I remember sitting on my couch and thinking, 'What the hell did I just do?'"

Brian put together about $23,000.

"Charlie Forsyth of West Coast Bank gave us the SBA loan," Molly says. "We met with Charlie to work out terms. Brian had to have a certain amount of money in. We thought it was enough.

"In the eleventh hour, as we were starting to sign leases and get customers, we got a call from Charlie. He said, 'I hate to tell you this; we're going to need more money from you.'"

The figure necessary: $63,000.

"Brian had taken out his 401K and his savings, and now it wasn't enough," Molly says. "He asked other people and got 'nos' from them."

Brian and Molly decided to turn to their last resort.

❄

On a Sunday afternoon in January 2002, they knocked on the Comers' door and told Frosty and wife Vicki they wanted to talk to them about a proposed new company.

"They had a business plan in a three-ring binder, and we sat around the kitchen table," Frosty says. "Brian said, 'We want to start a company. We need to borrow some money. Here is our business plan.'"

Frosty, who had been in business for the better part of three decades, listened. Then he set aside the plan.

"Brian, of all the businesses started this year, you would be lucky if 50 percent are there after two years, and 75 percent are gone after five years," Frosty said. "Let's talk about corporate culture and how and why businesses fail."

"Having experienced several start-up businesses and projects, both successful and not, I had developed a personal formula for what differentiates failing and successful businesses," Frosty says today.

FROSTY'S NO SNOWMAN

The four of them discussed the subject for at least 30 minutes.

"I emphasized the need to treat employees well, take excellent care of your customers and give back to your community," Frosty says. "Without those 'three legs of the stool,' a business will fail over time. Success revolves on those pillars. It's the bedrock of success."

The response from Brian and Molly: "We agree with that culture. We will live by that culture. We want to be that culture." Then they asked if they could borrow the money Brian needed to qualify for the SBA loan. The figure was $30,000.

Frosty was Coram's national vice president for Federal Health Services and Vicki was successful in her real estate position.

"But we were just getting out from paying the kids' college bills," Frosty says. "We had refinanced our house three times to pay for weddings and college. We were just getting out from under all of that.

"I said, 'No, we are not going to loan you any money.' I said it that way on purpose, for shock value. They looked like, 'What are we going to do now?' I waited 15 seconds and said, 'I will tell you what we are going to do.'"

Frosty proposed that he and Vicki provide them the $30,000 to start the business. In exchange, Frosty and Vicki would get 10 percent ownership of the company. In addition, Frosty would become chairman of the board, and Vicki one of its directors.

"When Vicki and I die, you will get an inheritance, anyway," Frosty told them. "If the business should fail, there is no need to pay us back. Let's go have some fun and make a difference. It's your job to run the company, but if you have any questions or issues, you better damn well come to me."

Says Frosty today: "Had it been a loan, they would have felt the pressure to pay us back. I wanted them to focus on making CSG a success."

Brian and Molly quickly agreed, and Molly set about creating the formal corporate documents that were required from the state of Oregon. The CSG SBA loan was approved.

"I asked a lot of people to invest in us," Brian says. "Frosty was the only one dumb enough to do it."

Smart enough, really.

"Ironically, we never touched the SBA loan," Brian says. "Right out of the gate, we were making money."

"When I filed the papers for ownership, my parents were on them," Molly says. "If we had lost it all, they would have lost it all. But that was the best move my parents ever made."

"No way," Frosty says. "Our best move was being their parents."

Brian secured the contracts he had previously negotiated at Mosler and Montec.

"We started with five employees, including two techs and an admin, me and my wife Shauna," Brian says. "I was slowly plucking away. I learned everything not to do working for those companies.

"Montec was slowly dying. Everybody there was calling me and saying, 'Bring me over there.' I said, 'I don't have the money yet. I am doing this as fast as I can.'"

Molly was not one of the CSG employees, not at first. She continued at Deloitte & Touche for nearly two more years. But she also continued to help Brian unpaid in the embryonic stages of Cook Security Group, even as she worked full-time at her day job with Deloitte. Molly didn't contribute any money to CSG, but Brian gave her a 10 percent stake in the company (which was increased to 15 percent about a year later).

"I gave Molly some sweat equity, for the hard work she put into it," Brian says. "Molly was critical. This company wouldn't be what it is without Molly's help, at first moonlighting with us."

Molly, still working full-time as a senior audit manager at Deloitte & Touche, took her meetings early in the week. On Fridays, she would put in a full day at the CSG office. She would come in at night sometimes to help out, too. She was learning the business.

As CSG added employees, Brian did some learning, too.

"We had a lot of fun nights in his office," Molly says. "I would be kidding him about how many cars he was going to buy. Every employee of ours had to help him understand the variable costs of the business. He had worked for larger companies. He had done what he was trained to do, but he managed by feel."

To start, CSG was about electronic banking security. "We didn't work in the ATM business at all at that point," Brian says. Fortunately, his previous relationships with customers paid off.

"If you go to a bank today, there is no way you get the loan we got," he says. "West Coast Bank invested in me because of our business plan, and I took that same plan to a lot of my customers. Remember, they had just gone through the Mosler and Montec debacles. And now they are going to do this again? I had some really good customers who believed in me. It was a big risk on their part."

Molly's first child, Joey, was born in September 2003. As she took maternity leave, she was contemplating whether to go back to Deloitte & Touche. Molly and Brian had a conversation.

"What are you thinking?" Brian asked. "You need to work for us."

At first, Molly said no.

"I can't do this without you," Brian said.

Molly talked it over with her husband, Aaron.

"We knew we wanted to have a couple of more kids," Molly says. "So I decided to quit Deloitte & Touche. We made the decision for the family."

She started working two days a week for CSG. Then three. Finally, in January 2004, she became a full-time employee.

The company grossed $1.2 million for its first full fiscal year of operation in 2002 and '03.

"Brian worked his butt off," Frosty says. "He was good with customers. He was driven. He was competitive. I like to think the time he spent with us during his high school years gave him that competitive spirit and desire to continue to be better every day."

Molly quit her job at Deloitte & Touche and began full-time at CSG in January 2004. During her first full year there, gross income reached $3.7 million.

❄

When CSG started, Frosty sought uniqueness.

"Having gone through a life full of business and clinical experiences, it became clear to me that if CSG wanted to compete against multi-million dollar national companies, it had to be different," he says. "Phil Knight's Nike slogan ("Just Do It") resonated with me, as well as the Army slogan ("Be All You Can Be")."

Brian, meanwhile, was looking to not repeat past mistakes. What lessons had Brian learned not to do from experiences at his first two places of employment?

"Greed, and lack of a plan," he says. "When Mosler went under, the Montec owner tripled his staff, thinking he was going to get all their contracts. But he didn't have any infrastructure or the accounting team. It slowly bit them; that is how they went under. Mosler was actually a profitable company, but was privately held, and the ownership kept sucking the cash out of it and getting high-interest loans to push cash into their pockets. The banks shut them down."

Within a couple of months, Cook began hiring employees.

"Hires were trickling in," he says. "Every month, we were hiring."

CSG was first housed in two offices and a tiny warehouse in Milwaukie, Ore.

"It didn't last long because we outgrew it quickly," Brian says.

Brian and Molly then bought a larger site in Milwaukie that was "company-owned" for the first time.

After outgrowing that facility, they financed and built a $9.5-million corporate office on NE Cascade Parkway near the Portland International Airport. They moved there in 2018.

Today, the company is called Cook Solutions Group. Brian is the company's majority owner and chief executive officer. Molly is chief financial officer. The company now has 418 employees. Gross income for the 2021 fiscal year: $115 million.

"The experience Brian has gone through is a re-do of what you read in Phil Knight's 'Shoe Dog,' with what Brian has been able to accomplish," Frosty says. "CSG is not a multi-billion dollar company like Nike, but it is a company that started with five employees and is now valued at $120 million."

❄

For the first few years of Cook Solutions Group's existence, the focus was on physical and electronic security. In 2006, CSG expanded its services to include selling and servicing ATMs in a larger, multi-state footprint. In 2008, the Cook Community Builders Program was launched, opening the door for charitable endeavors and community service. In 2009, the company developed "RemoteView," a service designed to increase its ability to service and monitor ATM and video surveillance products.

By 2012, CSG was offering an annual "SOC 2" type audit to its customers. In 2014, it added "Interactive Teller" to its solutions suite. In recent years, "Piko VMS" was invented — the future of surveillance.

In 2018 came the state-of-the-art headquarters and technology center.

"Our senior management team was heavily involved with the design," Brian says. "Our architects were really good. It was a heck of a project working with the Port of Portland, the city of Portland and the state of Oregon."

It took two years for permits to be approved, four years for construction to be completed.

"That was wild," Brian says. "It was a very complicated transaction. We had to go all the way to the mayor and his assistant to get the property. It is leased by the city of Portland but owned by the airport. Port of Portland representatives were sitting on it. It was frustrating, because taxpayers were paying for this land. I was like, 'Hey, we offer a lot of jobs and a lot of opportunity.' We finally were able to do it, but not in timely fashion."

Cook and his senior managers designed the building to be a place where employees want to hang out. There is a workout room, a picnic area, even a band room.

"Some of our people like to head in there about 4 p.m. every Friday and wind down," Brian says. "We have six to 10 employees who participate. They bring their guitars back there and jam."

In 2021, Cook Security Group became Cook Solutions Group, due to its expanding sphere of problem-solving and customer service in the technology space.

"It is more adapted to what we are offering now, with all the technology and products that we are developing," Brian says. "It is more than just banking security now. We wanted to rebrand and refresh it."

CSG has 15 branches and serves nearly 23,000 locations in 12 states physically. It also has 20 value added resellers (VARs small security/ATM companies) selling its software solutions and its managed services.

"So technically, we are nationwide," Brian says.

CSG monitors more than 100 million transactions each year on ATMS, working with such companies as Wells Fargo banks, Oregon Community Credit Union, Asante Health System, Cuna Mutual Group and the Portland Timbers.

In 2021, Inc. 500 ranked CSG 4,282nd among the nation's 5,000 fastest growing private companies.

In 2022, CSG won the prestigious Partner of the Year Award from NCR Platinum Solution Provider.

From 2009 through 2021, CSG was annually ranked among the top 32 best companies to work for in Oregon by Portland Business Journal. Five times it has ranked among the top 20.

"It is wonderful to be recognized for all these awards, but getting the 'Best Company to Work For' Awards make me the most proud, since it verifies the culture we set out to achieve," Frosty says. "My formula is the same as Einstein's: $E=MC^2$, Excellence = Members (employees), Customers and Community."

Since 2019, CSG has experienced gross revenue growth of 38 percent.

"Never in our wildest dreams did we think we would be where we are today," Molly says.

CHAPTER 14

BRIAN'S SONG AN INSPIRATIONAL ONE

To gain clients, executives at Cook Security Group, later to become Cook Solutions Group, have had to be creative.

Sometimes, they draw on past relationships.

When CEO Brian Cook and Molly Angelo visited administrators with the Beaverton School District to pitch their security plan, they wore their Beaverton High letterman jackets. They got the job.

Cook, Angelo, company president John Brase, chief marketing officer Randy Neu and chief experience officer Craig Cook are among those who are Beaverton High alumni. It is called "connections."

Sometimes, there are hurdles to clear. Big ones.

In 2014, as CSG was becoming bigger, an Ohio-based company named Diebold filed a federal lawsuit, a complaint for copyright infringement, misappropriation of trade secrets, breach of contract and patent infringement. In reality, it was a case of a multi-billion dollar company trying to kill off a smaller, emerging competitor.

"It was painful," Brian says. "It was the David vs. Goliath thing. We were taking so much business from them."

CSG had opened branches in cities such as Seattle, Boise, Sacramento and Reno.

"We partnered with companies and they would be our re-sellers," Frosty Comer says. "Diebold saw us as a big threat in the West. They were trying to take us down.

"They were harassing us with the lawsuit. They were trying to get our legal expenses so high that we couldn't continue. I told Brian, 'You have to be a wolf and mark your territory.'"

Says Brian: "They charged that we were stealing proprietary information from them, servicing their ATMs that we were not allowed to, and that some of their former employees whom we hired brought over proprietary information. It was all a bunch of BS to slow us down. I had never been through a situation of that magnitude."

After an investigation, representatives from CSG's insurance company said it wouldn't cover any losses CSG would incur in the legal complaint.

"We threatened to sue the insurance company," Cook recalls.

When the insurance company reps caught wind of CSG's intentions, they reversed course, saying they indeed would cover any judgments.

"When Diebold found out about that, they dropped the suit," Brian says.

The judge had sent the case to arbitration. Brian and Molly had plane tickets to Cincinnati to meet with Diebold when word came of the turn of events.

"They decided to settle," Brian says. "We agreed to pay a licensing fee. Our entire cost was probably about $50,000. They were suing us for millions."

"What was hilarious was that Diebold decided they still needed CSG to sell and service some of their products," Frosty says. "That was a huge win. They were the Amazon of the security world.

"It is an evil part of the corporate world, when a big company can harass and drive a small company out of business via a frivolous lawsuit. It was one of the more significant challenges Brian and Molly faced."

Competition from other companies has lessened over the years. Few have been able to keep the pace of CSG.

"A lot of them are gone," Brian says. "A lot of them didn't grow like we were growing. I knew we had to get in multiple states and grow faster throughout the 12 Western states. Much of the competition stayed status quo and didn't adapt to the industry. A lot of these banks acquire other banks and go into multiple states. That was key for our growth."

Brian is a sports fan. So are many of those who work under him at CSG. One of the fringe benefits of having a successful business is being able to afford a few luxuries. The company has four club seats for Trail Blazers games at Moda Center, often used by employees or customers. It also owns season tickets for Timbers and Thorns soccer games at Providence Park.

Cook wants CSG to grow, both in numbers and in quality of output.

"I don't know how you run a company if you are not growing," he says. "I equate it to sports. I don't want to be in second place; I want to be in first place. I see us continuing to grow. We may grow in different departments with our technology. I have too much competitive spirit in me. I can't slow down."

Throughout his career, Brian has learned that honesty is the best policy.

"Being real, that's the No. 1 thing," he says. "A lot of customers say I am the worst salesman. I am very transparent, both with customers and our employees."

Brian has recently been mentoring a pair of friends of his son Brandon.

"It has been fun," he says. "I like showing them the ropes of this industry."

What kind of advice does he offer?

"It is hard work," Brian says. "Nothing is easy. A lot of kids expect to make it big in a year or two, but it takes years. It takes dedication and drive to get there."

Frosty believes Brian's song is an inspirational one.

"A kid with two years of community college is the majority owner and CEO of a $120 million company," Frosty marvels. "This is a great story for kids who may not be a fit for four years of college. I am not so big on college anymore, even though I have multiple degrees. I've started telling kids they should probably go to community college for two years instead of racking up a bunch of debt.

"Brian is a classic case of someone who has made an incredible business out of nothing. If that is not inspirational, I am not sure what is."

Has success changed the man atop the corporate ledger at CSG?

"Don't think so," Cook says with a smile. "Still the same old Brian."

After working with Cook for more than two decades, Angelo is a believer in Brian's leadership.

"Brian is the idea guy," she says. "He gets 100 percent of the credit. He is very well-respected in the security industry. People trust him because he is an honest guy. That is why all of his old customers moved over to us when we started.

"A lot of businesses fail in the first months or years. We never had those growing pains. Everybody followed Brian over because they believed in him, believed that he was doing the right thing, and that he would do right by them. It has been our reputation. For many years, we never had a sales or marketing team. It was by word of mouth and reputation that we would grow."

There are other reasons for CSG's success.

"I would point to the strong culture we have created, and that we really care about our customers and employees," Molly says. "It is an industry that weathers the storms. Security is vital to protect people and money, especially during hard times. We haven't taken the company for granted. We have tried to do the right thing by our customers and employees. So far, it has worked well. The larger you get, the harder it is. You are only as good as your weakest link. We have done a good job of identifying and hiring the right people.

"We hire a lot of families and friends. It has worked really well for us for the most part. We take care of each other. We trust each other. We work hard for each other. But we also have learned you can't always just hire family and friends."

Only 25 percent of CSG's employees are women. Part of that is it is a male-dominated industry. Women, though, play a major role in the company's brand. Molly's nine years of experience at Deloitte & Touche accounting firm gave her insight into how to help make that happen.

"Deloitte was such a family-friendly company, especially toward women," she says. "They were ahead of their time in terms of doing flex schedules and allowing employees to work from home. Here I was able to offer that to many employees, where the job allowed for it.

"If you want to hire and retain talented people, that is important. A lot of the people I have hired are women coming back to the work force later in life. These were some of the things they wanted and needed. We have been that way for many years."

❄

One of the most important aspects of CSG is Cook Community Builders, a program instituted as a conduit for community outreach. It is an internal company volunteer program in which full-time employees can annually use 16 hours — two full days — of company-paid time to assist in a local community activity, such as charities, Red Cross, Oregon Food Bank, etc.

"Each project has to be approved," Molly says, "but we have become pretty flexible. A ton of our donation requests come to me from our employees for causes that they or their children are involved in. We donate money for customers' golf tournaments and other events. There are a lot of those that happen every year."

"It is a $200,000 annual investment," Frosty says, "but it is a passion of ours, and particularly Brian."

"I love it," Brian says. "It is important that we give back, and we do it in a lot of ways."

Over the years, CSG has worked with such non-profit pursuits as Children's Miracle Network, Credit Union for Kids, Walk for the Cure and the Hood to Coast run. For eight years, CSG contributed to "Tools for School," which provides free school supplies to under-resourced students and classrooms.

"Our employees would take a day and fill backpacks to deliver to students on the first day of school," Molly says. "We provided it for every student regardless of need. That is the fair way to do it."

CSG has donated lumber, equipment and work forces for De

La Salle North Catholic, a faith-based, college prep high school for underserved students from the Portland area. CSG contributed to a construction project for a community center for the elderly.

Participation in the program is not required. "About 20 percent of our employees take advantage of all 16 hours," Molly says.

A particular favorite activity of the Cook Community Builders is donating manpower and supplies to assist the Slingball Tournament it stages each summer at Pacific City. The 16th annual event will be held in June 2023. The charity is Multiple Sclerosis, with proceeds going to the Marilyn Neu Memorial Fund, named in honor of the mother of CSG employees Randy and Carter Neu. Marilyn Neu died of complications from the disease in 2005.

"It is an important cause," says Brian Cook, who has played in all 16 tournaments. "There are a lot of rivalries, and it is competitive. But there are friendships in the rivalries."

Slingball is a yard game that is a little bit horseshoes, a little bit cornhole, a little bit bocce ball and a lot of fun.

"Hillbilly golf, cowboy golf … there are so many names for Slingball," says Randy Neu, who with brother Carter Neu serves as co-chairs of the non-profit Slingball, Inc. "You kind of sling it like a gunslinger, so we named it that."

A foot-long piece of rope is tied with a pair of recycled golf balls — one at each end. The player slings the implement to land on a small tower (made of PVC pipe) with four crossbars some 25 feet away. Points are awarded. First to 21 wins.

Carter discovered the game while attending a Lincoln City Elks Club picnic with a girlfriend years ago.

"Her grandpa was playing the game, so we started playing it," Carter says. "Later, I made my own set and added a back bar, and we played in our backyard for a while. Everyone was calling it 'Hang ball.' "

After Marilyn died, "Carter and I were trying to think of something to do so we could remember her," Randy says. "At the same time, we were playing this crazy game that we now called 'Slingball.' So, we said, 'How about a tournament that raises money for MS?' And Slingball was founded."

Boys and girls and men and women of all ages compete in an event that has now raised nearly a quarter of a million dollars for charity through the years.

"Our company is about community involvement, and that is what this event is about," says Frosty, who never misses a tournament. "There are some people who have played every event since the beginning, and many more who have participated for many years. It has become a big Slingball family. They are here for the fun of the game, but also to support the charity."

Part of the fund-raising effort is a silent auction, which offers many featured items. The No. 1 prize of the weekend, however, is the "Slingball Cup" and green jackets that go to the winners of each division. Tournament tradition calls for the overall champion to fill the Slingball Cup with his/her favorite beverage and chug it.

"It is usually beer," Carter says. "One year, one of the winners was an LDS member — a non-drinker. He poured the beer from the cup into the mouth of the previous year's winner."

CHAPTER 15

Treating Employees and Customers Right

Through the doors of Cook Solutions Group have come a variety of employees who have been instrumental in the growth and success of a family-owned business.

Among them is Wendy Lambert, eldest daughter of Frosty and Vicki Comer.

Wendy has been with CSG since 2009 following a career in education and real estate.

A 1991 Oregon State graduate in human growth and development, Wendy married in 1992, got her teaching credentials and Masters degree from Pacific University in the fall of '92.

She landed a full-time job at Beaverton's Five Oaks Middle School in 1994 and taught sixth grade full-time for four years. Once she had a son, Zachary, in 1998, she job-shared and taught part-time for the next three years. When her second son, Blake, was born in 2001, she took a year's leave of absence from teaching. Then in 2003, she joined her mother in real estate.

"I didn't like it," Wendy says. "If I could have been full-time and gotten into it, it might have been all right, but I was doing it as a supplemental thing so I could be home for my kids."

In 2009, sister Molly Angelo, the company's CFO, offered her a position at CSG. For six months, Wendy divided her time between CSG and real estate before she turned to CSG full-time. Fourteen years later, she is still at CSG, currently serving as an agreement and account analyst manager.

"I like it," Wendy says. "I have done a lot of different things since I started, but I have always been with the accounting department. I get to see Molly a lot more, and I like the team I work with. The job is challenging, very detail-oriented, and that is me."

Wendy gives Brian and Molly high marks in leading the company to a pattern of growth and success.

"They have made us a company that puts the customer and employees first," Wendy says. "You hire employees and treat them well and help them see how important the customer is. Our main priority is to take good care of our customers.

"At Cook, we work hard and play hard, and we have a family environment. Molly provides an awesome work-and-fun balance for the employees. If you have any kind of family or personal matters to be taken care of, you can work on your own hours as long as you get the job done."

❄

Craig Cook is CSG's "chief experience officer," or as he puts it, vice president of operations. He focuses on providing good service and overall customer satisfaction. He is Brian's younger brother, two years his junior.

"Younger, but a lot better-looking," Craig jokes.

After a stint as an electronics technician in the Navy — "five years, eight months and 10 days," he says — Craig worked 13 years at Intel before joining the CSG staff in 2010. He started as the firm's first training manager and also served as service manager and general manager.

Currently, Cook and President John Brase split responsibilities.

"John oversees four of our centers; I oversee the other four," Craig says. "I oversee the data center, heavy equipment and the tech support team, and we split duties with the training department."

Craig sees "a couple of things" as keys to CSG's success.

"In a bit of a niche business, we have been able to grow with limited competition," he says. "The way we operate, we make it happen. When I was outside looking in, that motto seemed a little corny to me. But when you immerse yourself within the organization and the culture, there is no other phrase that would speak to what we do.

"The culture is good. For the longest time, we were a part of something bigger than us. It was us against the world, which brings challenges. Now we have the target on our back instead of the other way around, which seems weird to a lot of us."

Craig has an insider's opinion on his brother's expertise in running CSG.

"Brian has a unique leadership style," he says. "He is not a cookie-cutter CEO by any means. He has challenges with public speaking, which some people find charming and others can poke a little fun at. He is a roll-up-the-sleeves kind of guy and wants to dig into everything, which can be good, but also can be frustrating at times when you are growing a company the size we have and want to focus on the strategic vision.

"Brian inherited a lot of this from our grandfather, Ralph Cook, an incredible businessman. Everything came naturally to him as far as business goes. Brian has the same thing going for him. He is not this book-smart guy, but his business instincts and ability to say, 'Screw it, we're doing it,' helps him out as well.

"Nobody is more passionate about CSG and the company than Brian. It shows how much he cares for everyone in the organization, maybe minus his little brother."

❄

Randy Neu and Brian Cook grew up together.

"Brian and I were pals, fun-loving teammates," Randy says.

Their fathers coached their youth soccer teams from fifth through eighth grade. In seventh and eighth grade, Randy and Brian attended Whitford Middle School with Erik Spoelstra, playing on the same youth basketball team in seventh and eighth grade. Father Jon Spoelstra was the coach. Jon went on to a long career as an executive for several NBA teams, including the Portland Trail Blazers. Erik recently completed his 15th season as head coach of the Miami Heat, with two NBA championships and more than 700 regular-season victories to his credit.

"Brian, Erik and I were all pretty close," Randy says. "We kept it light, but we were serious when we needed to play hard."

Randy graduated from Beaverton High in 1988 and from the University of Oregon in 1992 in sports marketing. For more than three years, he worked as golf services manager at Red Tail Golf Course in Beaverton. He moved to the Hawaiian Islands and, for two months, sold season tickets for the Honolulu Sharks minor league baseball team. Then he was hired by the Trail Blazers as corporate sales manager, a job he held for 10 years until CSG beckoned.

"It was a seesaw ride with the Blazers," Neu says. "We went from Jail Blazers to making the Western Conference finals and then back to Jail Blazers again. Just after I left, we got the No. 1 pick in the draft — Greg Oden."

Randy says he enjoyed most of his job with the Blazers.

"I loved that we were putting on a show all the time," he says. "I loved the entertainment part of it, that it served as our customers' release. But it was a difficult time for the franchise, with all that was happening with our players. We always sold out until about 2002, but then people started getting fed up, we started to lose, and we lost a significant chunk of our season ticket-holders.

"It made it harder for us, but it made us tougher, too. We likened the experience to getting kicked in the teeth. Then it was a matter of selling the fact that it's still fun to go to games even if you aren't good."

Randy married wife Tracy on New Year's Eve 1997. They have two boys, Lucas and Ramsay — named after former Blazer power forward Maurice Lucas and ex-Blazer coach Jack Ramsay.

Neu had talked with Brian about starting CSG as far back as 2001. Randy won a trip to Hawaii in a sales contest with the Blazers and took Brian along. They stayed in former assistant coach John Wetzel's condo there.

"We were sitting on the beach, and we started seriously talking about Brian starting a business," Randy recalls.

"I love the idea, but are you sure you really want to do this?" Randy asked.

"I'm a little nervous about having to get a loan to get started," Brian said. "I know I'll be putting my ass on the line."

"If you are confident it can work," Randy said, "you gotta do it."

Randy wasn't looking to leave his job with the Blazers.

"By 2006, though, Brian had grown the business to the tipping point where he needed good, trustworthy people to help him," he says. "He told me, 'This is starting to get away from me; I need some support.'

"I had experience working in ticket and corporate sales with the Blazers. I could help out in some ways Brian needed help. My attitude was, 'Let's go grow something new. Neu serves as CSG's chief marketing officer.

"I used to be a road warrior, traveling to different states to help grow the business and tell the story," he says. "My role now is from the marketing standpoint — telling our story using social and digital media and spreading the word about our company. It has been an unbelievable ride. It is very fulfilling to see where we came from to where we are today, and we are still growing.

"People ask us our secret sauce; it is not that difficult if you do the right things. The secret is shooting straight, treating people like you want to be treated, and ultimately taking care of customers. That is really Brian's mantra, his identity. It is what he is all about. That is really what fuels CSG. We all have the same sort of morals and makeup, but it starts with him."

The company started with physical locations in Oregon and Washington. It is now in 12 states.

"We are national with our 'Value-added Reseller' program," Neu says. "We have gone beyond security, which is a strong backbone of our company and will never go away. But we offer so many more solutions. We go to customers and listen to their problems and come up with solutions. That's how we have grown. We are good listeners. As we continue to keep doing that, things open up. It perpetuates our growth."

❄

Teresa Salazar has seen much of CSG's growth. When she began as Human Resources manager 12 years ago, the payroll covered fewer than 100 employees.

"We have had such steady growth since then," Salazar says.

Teresa attended Oregon State but graduated from PSU's school of business. She was promoted to CSG's vice president/human resources in 2018.

"My focus is on the strategic side of things, the employee experience," she says. "I also oversee other things, from recruiting strategies to on-boarding strategies to technology and training."

Teresa is pleased that CSG's retention rate for employees is between 87 and 92 percent.

"We are definitely above the average," she says. "It feels like we are hiring the right people and being able to retain them. We have promoted between 30 to 35 positions each year.

"It is cool to be part of that culture, of who we are as a company — caring about people for who they are and what they can contribute, making sure we hire talent that is going to be a good fit for Cook, people naturally focused on doing the right thing for the customer."

Salazar has known chairman of the board Frosty Comer since she began at CSG. In 2020, she did a road trip to Corvallis with Frosty to provide Oregon State students — many of them of color — with an overview of CSG and to promote some job openings.

"It was nice for Frosty to provide support with that presentation," she says. "He cares about the company's success. He has been invested since the days it opened its doors. He is always looking forward to participating or providing some opportunity when it comes to giving back to the community."

Teresa is appreciative of the leadership at the top.

"Brian knows the industry in and out," she says. "He is a huge believer in including everybody as part of the team. He is big on teamwork, and that shows in his decision-making. People look up to him for that. Every single person in CSG contributes to the success of the company.

"He is focused on where we are going and allows our managers to help provide the strategic things. He truly cares about doing the right thing for the customer."

❄

John Brase is another Beaverton High grad who played Little League baseball with Randy Neu. After graduating from the University of Oregon, he worked in the route services industry for 10 years before being hired at CSG in 2008. John started as the firm's general manager for Oregon before being promoted to president and chief operating officer.

"I handle everything operationally, overseeing the different centers and their performance, as well as several key departments, from purchasing to training and different aspects there," Brase says.

John remembers speaking with Neu before he was hired.

"This is a dysfunctional little company, but there is something special going on here," Randy told him.

"We were a lot smaller then, but I valued having a family-owned, self-funded company, where you really felt you could make a difference," John says. "In comparison to my previous job, it is like steering a dinghy instead of the Titanic.

"We are still nimble and can adjust quickly. The 'what to do' is not hard to do; the execution is what is hard. We genuinely care about our employees and our customers. It is not always easy, but as long as you do that, profitability and performance will come. That has held true for 20 years at CSG."

Brase works closely with Cook.

"Brian is not your typical CEO," John says. "He is one of the most humble business owners I have met in my life. He doesn't have a big ego, and he is not the guy out there giving speeches and presentations all the time. He is a man of few words.

"But he has incredible business sense and a vision for where the industry is going. He is the key to helping us stay on the cutting edge. And he puts his faith in people."

Three months into employment at CSG, Brase checked in with Cook and asked, "What do you need me to work on?"

"I need you to make decisions," Brian answered. "I trust you to do that."

"He empowers the people he trusts, in that they will get us where we need to go," John says.

John is glad Frosty Comer is on board.

"I love Frosty," he says. "He has a huge heart. If he is passionate about something, he is full go. Most of Frosty's career success was outside of CSG. But to see him from the lens of being part of CSG, he always has his eyes and ears open, and if he feels there is an opportunity to meet with a potential customer or do something unique, he is always game for that."

Brase isn't the only one at CSG who appreciates Frosty's presence.

"Every year we have a corporate year-end party," Frosty says. "When I attend, a lot of people don't know who I am initially. If they do, they come up to me and say, 'I can't thank you enough. I so much enjoy working for Cook Security. You take care of us.'"

Frosty's response: "The more you invest in people, it's amazing what comes back."

FROSTY'S NO SNOWMAN

Brian Cook, Chief Executive Officer

Molly Angelo, Chief Financial Officer

John Brace, President

Randy Neu, Chief Marketing Officer

Scott Fieber, Chief Strategy Officer

Craig Cook, Chief Experience Officer

Levi Daily, Chief Technology Officer

Daniel Smallwood, Chief Operating Off.

Frosty Comer, Chairman

Chapter 16

Exploring the Better Half

Randy Neu, Chief Marketing Officer

Vicki Comer is the unsung hero of the Comer family.

The wife of Frosty Comer and mother of Wendy Lambert and Molly Angelo is a fortress in a land of strong personalities.

"Vicki is the anchor of our family," Frosty says. "She held everything together for us while I was working all these years."

And indeed, she was working herself.

After a decade with Far West Federal Bank, Vicki started work as a realtor at Lutz Snyder in 1990. Five years later, Snyder and Stan Wiley merged and they became Prudential Northwest Properties. In 2012, Prudential became Berkshire Hathaway HomeServices Northwest.

Thirty-three years after she started in real estate, Vicki is still at it.

"I am a very loyal person," she says. Those at Berkshire Hathaway "have been very good to me. I like the people I work with. I like the people in charge. I like their programs and what they have to offer. I like that they are very much a philanthropical company.

"I love helping people. There is never a dull moment. Every transaction is different. I love learning, and you learn something new every day in real estate."

Vicki spent most of her career as an agent. In 2019, she was named recipient of the Broker Excellence Award for Berkshire Hathaway, given annually to just one of the company's 900 agents.

"Vicki is a professional realtor in every way, but a better person than she is a realtor," says Bert Waugh, former owner and president of Prudential and Berkshire Hathaway. "She is an incredibly talented, quality individual."

In 2019, Vicki served four to five months as an interim branch manager before a full-time manager was hired. In 2021, he departed, and Vicki became interim branch manager again. A few months later, she took over the job full-time.

"I don't love to go out and recruit, but I love to help the agents," Vicki says. "I have all the knowledge. That is what I love about my job now. And I am still selling real estate, though not as much as before."

Vicki oversees about 50 agents who work in four branches in Oregon.

"I think she is phenomenal," says Jason Waugh, Bert's son and now president of Berkshire Hathaway. "Vicki is a positive force. She is never down, always upbeat and optimistic. She is a real asset to a sales organization from an attitude perspective. She is a great human being, friend, mom, grandmother, great grandmother and wife. She is also a darn good card player and golfer who leads a very active lifestyle with family and friends."

Larry Ross is the first boy who slept with Vicki, but that requires further explanation.

"It was in fourth grade," says Ross, a lifelong friend who is a former economics professor at Alaska-Anchorage. "My parents went on a business trip to Ashland and Vicki and I shared a bed. We were best friends. We met in 1953 when we were six years old. The Leiningers were our next-door neighbors in North Bend. Vicki and I were close friends and have stayed in touch ever since.

"She is a wonderful person. What you see is what you get. She is not one bit artificial or phony. She always has a positive attitude. I have never heard her say a negative thing about anybody. That is the kind of person she is. She is true blue."

In 1991, Bert Waugh began a non-profit "with the concept of feeding transitional youths, housing them, helping them with independent living and then home ownership," he says.

The program began in downtown Portland in 1993 and continued until 2020, when Covid and the riots hit. There currently are two houses in Clark County, Wash., one in Wilsonville and one in Damascus for young adults and unwed mothers.

"We get them off the streets and out of foster care, treatment centers or jail," Waugh says. "Vicki and Frosty have done a lot for the program over the years, as individuals and with their company (Cook Solutions Group). Both of them have huge hearts."

Vicki has served on the grievance committee for Portland Metropolitan Association of Realtors and, in 2018, acted as chairman.

"We are dealing with ethics, or lack thereof," she says. "There are a lot of people who are ethical, but you are not going to find anybody more ethical than me. That is very important to me — to be honest, up front, to tell the truth, admit you are wrong or if you don't know something."

Vicki has great respect for her daughters, who both work at Cook Solutions Group.

"They both bring a lot to the table," she says. "Wendy and Molly are a lot alike, but they have a lot of differences as far as personalities. Wendy is more outgoing, more exuberant. She has more of a personality like a schoolteacher than Molly. Molly is a CPA, but she is not stuffy. She is the best mom you are ever going to find. She is also very knowledgeable in what she does.

"That is why the people at CSG get along so well, because she makes sure everything goes smoothly. They are very good sisters; they're very good friends."

Ask Wendy for the first word that comes to mind with her parents, and the answer comes quickly.

"With Mom, loyalty," she says. "She is very loyal. Loving. With Dad, passionate. Also generous, very generous. Always looking at ways he can help people around him. Patriotic. Both of them are very proud and involved with family. Both would be there at the drop of a hat for anything their children or grandchildren need."

The Comers have been married 55 years for many reasons.

"Besides loving each other to death all those years, we are a great team," Frosty says. "We complement each other. She has always stepped up when I need her for anything. She is everything to me, emotionally as well as spiritually. We are Christians, though we have not been regular church-goers, until recently. But if a grandkids' game comes up, that takes precedent. She still loves working. I am not going to tell her to stop working.

"Vicki is everything to me. She is an amazing wife, amazing mother and an amazing sports fan."

Don't minimize that last attribute. The Comers had season tickets for the Trail Blazers for 45 years, ending with the 2021-22 season. They have season tickets for Oregon State football and basketball and go to some Beaver baseball games. They went with the OSU men's basketball team to France and Spain in 2012 and to Italy in 2022. The Comers are major donors to the OSU athletic department.

"Sports is what has connected us most," Frosty says. "Our world revolves around our grandkids and Beaver sports. What has been really fun for us is a lot of the OSU basketball players, such as Roberto Nelson, have become surrogate grandkids to us."

Ask Vicki what has made her and Frosty such a good couple for so long, and get a succinct, honest response.

"Marriage is about give and take," she says. "You can't take, take, take. With both of us, we have given and taken. It is a combination thing. We agree to disagree sometimes. We have a lot of the same likes. The thing that drew us together is sports. It is one of our main interests. We are always involved in activities that include sports.

"We tease each other. We have fun together. Frosty was very good with my mother after my dad died. He has been a wonderful husband. I know he deeply loves me, and he shows it all the time. He has always had my back and supported me with anything and everything I have done."

Vicki & Larry Ross, 1954

FROSTY'S NO SNOWMAN

Vicki & Frosty at a Beaver Football Game

Vicki & Frosty on the Oregon Coast

Frosty & Vicki at a 4th of July Golf Tournament

CHAPTER 17

Frosty — 'A Single Name, Like Madonna'

The love Frosty and Vicki Comer have for Oregon State — and in particular, its sports teams and its school of pharmacy — runs deep.

In 2005, Frosty wanted to memorialize the military service of his paternal grandfather in World War I, his father and Vicki's father in World War II and his own time serving 4 1/2 years during Vietnam and five months during the first Gulf War, along with 22 years of service in the active Army Reserve. He and Vicki established the Comer Family Endowment at the Oregon State College of Pharmacy. Since that time, they have awarded scholarships for students who have served, or are serving, in the military. Last year, two students — Tyler Bishop and Gloria Zepeda — received $2,500 scholarships.

"In addition, each year, we and other donors financially support the students who attend the annual Joint Federal Pharmacy seminar, where they can get career counseling and attend several educational sessions presented by the military, the VA and other organizations," Frosty says.

Frosty accompanies the students — always with a military connection — to the annual seminar. In 2022, he took Bishop, on a Navy scholarship, and Zepeda, an enlisted Air Force human resource technician, to the seminar in Cleveland, paying for their flights and hotel. And more than that, mentoring them.

"It is a chance for them to get some career counseling, to interact with pharmacists and pharmacy technicians to see what a pharmacy career would be like in the military, public health service or the VA," Frosty says. "Not all of them choose those organizations, but it is great to see some of our scholarship recipients who are now senior pharmacy managers in the military or VA systems."

Frosty is an affiliate faculty member of the OSU College of Pharmacy and "preceptor" for students — a non-paid faculty member who can be called on to provide educational opportunities and lectures.

The Comer Family Endowment, now with a base of $110,000, gives between one and three scholarship awards a year. One of the first recipients was Brian Zacher, a Clackamas High grad who is now a civilian pharmacist living in Tualatin and is the pharmacy manager at the local Fred Meyer pharmacy. Zacher, a graduate of the OSU College of Pharmacy, served an initial three-year active duty tour out of high school with the 82nd Airborne Army unit stationed in Fort Bragg, N.C. He then joined the Oregon National Guard before attending Oregon State and was deployed once to Iraq and once to Afghanistan in 2004 and '05.

Zacher met Frosty through the process of applying for a Comer Family Endowment scholarship.

"They provided a financial scholarship that repeated from year to year, but it also opened doors to military pharmacies," says Zacher, now retired from the National Guard "We went to joint forces seminars and got to meet some very senior active-duty pharmacy leaders, and I was able to do a pharmacy clerkship rotation at Madigan Army Medical Center at Fort Lewis in Tacoma, Wash. As part of my pharmacy school rotations, I got to work at military treatment facilities."

Says Comer: "Brian is probably the only Command Sergeant Major in the history of the U.S. military who is a pharmacist."

Zacher has a great deal of gratitude for the help he received.

"Frosty is a very remarkable man," he says. "He is intelligent, social, caring, supportive. Very outgoing. He is civic-minded, family-oriented, energetic — all positive things.

"He is so involved, so networked. He is always looking to introduce people to each other and have mutually supportive and beneficial relationships. He has so much passion for Oregon State, the students, the athletes. He has a genuine, sincere caring for all of their well-being."

❄

Joey Jenkins is a 2007 OSU grad with a Masters degree. In 2010, Frosty hired him to be a personal trainer for him at a 24-Hour Fitness Club. They worked together for three or four years.

"Joey is incredible," Frosty says. "He is part of a group of OSU students that started the Oregon division of a non-profit group called 'NCompass.' They put on once-a-month lunches for homeless kids in Portland."

The non-profit is now the primary sponsor for the Maranatha House, an orphanage in Haiti. Due to Frosty's relationship with Joey, CSG has gotten involved as a major sponsor, helping to improve the security around the orphanage compound and donating Rosetta Stone English cassettes and laptops.

Joey and wife Stephanie are chairs of the Oregon division of NCompass and started a counseling business for teenagers and young adults. Joey got a contract with Oregon Youth Authority to work with kids at MacLaren Youth Correctional Facility. The kids in the program had earned the right to participate in the group called "The Influencers."

Once a week, Joey would present lectures on life skills, life planning and other topics. The majority of the youths signed up for the GED program to obtain their high school degrees. A number of them registered for community college classes, and a few were working on college degrees, such as Noah Schultz, who ended up getting two degrees from Oregon State.

For a couple of years, before COVID cut the access to the facility, Frosty attended the meetings with Joey and delivered a lecture to the students. He donated more than 20 copies of one of his favorite inspirational books, Tom Peters' "Thriving on Chaos," and used a chapter at a time to deliver a message of creating positive opportunities during chaotic times.

❄

After Frosty retired from Coram in 2011, his work career wasn't entirely finished. He served the company two more years as a consultant, then consulted for a group called Home Solutions from 2014-17, and in 2020 and '21 for Amerita, also a home infusion company.

But he had more time to get involved with Oregon State athletics. In 2012, he became a member of the board of Our Beaver Nation, the fundraising arm of OSU athletics. He became secretary in 2015, president-elect in 2017 and served as president from 2019-21.

On the board, Frosty was a doer.

"The first couple of years, I was getting very discouraged," he says. "We would go to a meeting and athletic director Bob De Carolis — who did some great things, and I do like him — would come in and tell us what he wanted us to hear. We would break into small groups and document things we wanted to have improved. We would have lunch, go to a sporting event that night, and that was it. Nothing much got done."

Earlier in this book, we heard Frosty refer to a military term, "force multiplier."

"That is, when you put tanks and infantry together — one plus one equals five," he says. "If you add artillery, one plus one plus one equals ten. I saw where Our Beaver Nation volunteer board could be a force multiplier in raising money and building alumni participation."

When Todd Stansbury took over as AD in 2015, with Jim Patterson as the OSU Foundation's senior associate director for development, things began to change.

"We started developing a committee structure to move on things we always thought needed to be improved," Frosty says.

Scott Barnes succeeded Stansbury as AD in late 2016. With help from Aaron Escobar, OSU's senior associate director for development, and Jeff Pivic, associate AD//senior director of annual and leadership giving, the 25-member OBN board has revised the board into a four-committee structure: Seating and parking, fund-raising strategy, communications and stewardship, and alumni engagement.

"We transformed the Our Beaver Nation advisory board to be the force multiplier for the athletic department's fund-raising and alumni engagement efforts," Frosty says. "For example, we developed a priority points program that turned seat selections into an objective instead of a subjective event. Instead of who you know, it is what are your priority points? We had to navigate through new tax laws and educate the alumni that if you take priority points you can't take tax deductions. We helped with the re-seating of Gill Coliseum during its renovation and the remodeling of the west side of Reser Stadium."

The fund-raising strategy committee was responsible for working with the athletic department's participation in "Dam Proud Day," the giving day for the university.

"The athletic department was the most successful fundraiser entity of all the colleges and programs in the university," Frosty says.

The communications and stewardship committee is responsible for reviewing all communication that are published by the OBN committees as well as the on-line quarterly newsletter that is sent to all alumni.

The alumni engagement committee reaches out to alumni, and especially young alumni, via events to get them engaged early on, even when they are still students.

Frosty enjoyed his time as president.

"It was rewarding and it was fun to be able to help create an entity that will continue, ensure that we stay current, and meet the needs of the athletic department and the alumni," he says. "We created the force multiplier for the foundation and the athletic department to be all they can be."

Frosty's work was appreciated by those in many departments at Oregon State.

"Frosty is a go-getter," Pivic says. "I don't know how he has so much energy. Both he and Vicki have a motor. There is not a challenge either of them shy away from."

Since he arrived at OSU in 2016, Pivic has overseen the Our Beaver Nation board of advisors.

"It is not a fiduciary board, just a board we look to in terms of fund-raising, philanthropy, parking issues and getting a fan's perspective," Pivic says. "It provides us a great window into what the people out there are thinking. To get somebody else's thoughts is very helpful to us. We have a book of business with people we have relationships with. We make sure we are cultivating and stewarding them. Because of Frosty's relationship on the board, he fell into my portfolio."

Pivic's first couple of years at OSU, he spoke with Comer on almost a daily basis.

"He really helped us with the board," Pivic says. "Prior to his presidency, it was meeting once a quarter and was primarily an update meeting. He helped us establish committees. We focus on financial sustainability and donor acquisition initiatives. He has helped it become a more professional organization. If you are a member, we don't want to just give you an update; we want to put you to work a little bit, get your thoughts on things. Without him, I don't know if we would have gotten there.

"He is retired on paper, but he keeps so busy with us, the College of Pharmacy and all of his other interests. He and Vicki are both highly motivated; always have been. They are passionate about Oregon State. They wear it on their sleeve. They are always trying to introduce me to people who can help Oregon State. We treat them like extended family members.

"And they are very generous. Their philanthropy is outstanding. I truly think Oregon State athletics is probably the first place they think of where they can help. They are creating a lot of opportunities for our student-athletes. They are special people to us."

❄

Paige Clark worked as director of alumni relations and professional development for OSU's College of Pharmacy from 2009-20. She is a 1986 grad of the OSU College of Pharmacy who worked extensively with Comer.

"Frosty was ever-present," says Clark, now a vice president for a pharmacy technology company. "I was his alumni director for 11 years and had the privilege of working with him on a number of college and student-related projects. Frosty has been extremely involved in relationships with students in the College of Pharmacy. He was always particularly supportive of those College of Pharmacy students who were also serving in a military capacity."

Comer is hands on because he knows that is the way things best get done. It is why OSU officials were quick to beckon his assistance, especially if the military is involved.

"Frosty was often my first phone call when we had students entering a College of Pharmacy class from one of the military branches," Clark says. "He would mentor them. He would be sure they were supported in any way he was able to provide support. It might be something like sponsoring their attendance at a conference, or something personal like keeping in close touch with them as a mentor, or just to check in multiple times a term to see how they were doing in their academic pharmacy pursuits.

"He also was very adept at gathering other alumni for various projects. As a huge athletic supporter at Oregon State, he was key in my outreach to widening circles of alumni that perhaps had not been back to the college in some years. I was grateful for his partnership and assistance in taking time to either make a phone call to reach out to alums or inviting them to come to the many events I hosted at the college. And then many times we would attend a football or basketball game together."

There is no need for a surname when Frosty is involved, Clark says.

"In the College of Pharmacy, we are a very close-knit family of professionals, and Frosty is known by many generations of pharmacists," she says. "It is kind of like having a single name like Madonna. It is Frosty. That is all you have to say. I leveraged his kindness and generosity, and I would be remiss if I did not include Vicki. She is one of the dearest souls and always would show up. She was always first in the door with a big hug and a smile. If I were hosting an alumni homecoming event, for instance, it would be Vicki in that door first."

When Clark took the job in 2009, there was no alumni program within the College of Pharmacy.

"In 11 years, we were able to build a whole program, a continuing education division, and there were a handful of alumni central to being there to support the college time and time again," Clark says. "The Comers were among that group. Not only are they fun — Vicki is the definition of fun — but we also threw 'Fan Cave' events."

In those events, alums would judge entrepreneurial projects from academy students.

"Frosty wasn't centrally engaged in that, but he always showed up," Clark says. "He and Vicki came and would bring friends. If I was selling tickets as a fundraiser to an event, they would be like, 'Great, we will take four and we will bring friends.' "

Clark understands that she is contributing to the story of someone who has made major contributions in many ways — and not just with capital. He doesn't do it alone, but he is at the head of the class.

"The tricky bit for me about this book is it is imperative that we frame this as Frosty being part of a central group of alumni," she says. "That is very true. A group of a dozen or so alumni equally contributed. They are the first to pick up the phone and say, 'How can I help you, Paige?' Frosty always picked up the phone. He never knew what urgency it might be. A couple of times, it was urgent. Those words came out of his mouth every time I called him.

"He takes service to his community seriously, and here is the thing that I think is really important to stress: Sometimes it is not just about the money. It is about what you have invested with yourself and your time. In the College of Pharmacy, that mentorship piece is priceless. Truly. It is great to have a scholarship, don't get me wrong, but it is not just about the money. It is a profession, and you must have guidance, some mentor relationship. Every single year, he would pick up more mentees — the students who were former military, current military or exploring serving in the military.

"There is an important lesson here for people to understand the importance of committing regularly to giving back to those coming after you. It is imperative to the health of any profession. Frosty and Vicki were premier alums in the respect of assuring that they are tending to the health of the profession."

In 2005, Frosty was honored as the winner of the E.B. Lemon Distinguished Alumni of the Year Award at Oregon State.

"I was blown away," he says. "I was on several great teams that had great folks that did some amazing innovations that contributed to the overall health of the school of pharmacy, the university and the community.

"The culture at Oregon State was what provided me with those opportunities. It gave me the chance to be creative and to have a great career along with an amazing family. I support sports and academics. When I hired people, if they had a great academic resume, I would ask, 'What else have you done? Have you played sports? Have you learned to be a team member?'

"Sports can teach you discipline, accountability, responsibility, how to win and lose, how to become part of a team. If I miss anything at my advanced age, it is the camaraderie you get from being on those teams. I also learned that the structure and the mission of the military is very similar to that of a sports team."

In 2007, another major award came Frosty's way. He was named an "Icon of Pharmacy" by Oregon State's school of pharmacy for his many contributions through the years, a practice that has continued through today.

Though he moved away from Taft High in Lincoln City, Ore., after his sophomore year, one of his favorite academic awards is an honorary degree that his Taft classmates bestowed on him.

"I have it framed in my house," he says.

He recently attended a 60th reunion celebration at Taft as well as a 60th anniversary of his baseball team at Wilson High.

"It is the kind of camaraderie that I have been fortunate to have throughout my life," Frosty says.

❄

The nine lives of Frosty Comer:

1) In 1956, age 12, a kidney infection in sixth grade that caused him to miss two months of school. The doctor said Frosty could have lost his kidneys if he hadn't started penicillin when he did. "I was treated with intramuscular procaine penicillin once a week for two months, then prophylactic oral penicillin for five years," he says. "Boy, did those weekly penicillin injections in my 12-year-old butt hurt. I couldn't walk for a couple of days."

2) In 1970, age 26, playing for the flag football Army hospital team in Vicenza Italy, an opponent threw an intentional forearm shiver and fractured his jaw. Frosty had oral surgery and his mouth was wired shut for six weeks. "People were happy about that, I'm sure," he cracks.

3) In 1980, age 36, on his 12th wedding anniversary, and the same day Mt. St. Helens volcano erupted, he had emergency surgery for a ruptured appendix. "I was in the hospital for 10 days while receiving triple antibiotic therapy," he says. "Had I waited any longer, the infection would have been systemic with a very poor potential outcome."

4) In 1993, age 49, Frosty had a coronary artery bypass graft surgery as a result of getting hit in the chest with an elbow in a basketball game in Medford. "My heart stopped and I was dead," Frosty says. "The doctor, who had just emerged from the athletic club's locker room, had to do CPR to save my life. I had double mammary bypass surgery a week later at Good Samaritan Hospital and was discharged after six days. I participated in cardiac rehab for two months afterward."

5) In 2011, age 67, Frosty experienced a severe ruptured disc that wasn't life-threatening but left his left leg paralyzed for about a week. "I couldn't walk," he says. "I finally got a steroid injection the following week. We were supposed to go on a golf trip to Scotland and England the week after. I recovered in time to be able to play St. Andrews."

6) In 2020, age 76, Frosty had a L3/4/5 laminectomy surgery to take pressure off of the nerve roots that kept getting pinched and paralyzed. "The recovery was difficult, and it took about two months to recover before I could play golf again," he says. "Every so often, I still need a steroid injection in this area to mitigate the pain and paralysis."

7) Also in 2020, Frosty's primary dentist, Dr. Fred Fischer, discovered oral squamous cell cancer. "On my tongue," he says. Successful surgery followed. "Luckily it was stage 1, with an 80 percent survival rate," Frosty says.

8) In 2021, age 77, Frosty experienced a severe pulmonary embolism in his lungs that required three days in intensive care at St. Vincent Hospital. It started on a flight to Eugene after an Oregon State football game at Purdue. "I ended up having a horrible case of vertigo," he says. "I threw up in the bathroom on the bus back to Corvallis. Felt bad for weeks until one day when breathing got extremely difficult. Vicki called 911 and I went via ambulance to St. Vincent Hospital, where they treated me for the embolism. I'm lucky I made it through that one."

FROSTY'S NO SNOWMAN

9) Frosty, who also underwent total knee replacement in late 2022 -- his 17th surgery overall -- knows he is fortunate to be alive. "I push the envelope," he says. "Sometimes I pay for it. You have to have the attitude that you are not going to let things stop you. I want to take advantage of every second we have to live, because it is so precious. You begin to wonder, why am I being saved all these times? God saved me for some reason. I am here to do things for people. That is why I was put on this earth."

To. Do. Things. "Jesus taught we are here to serve, not be served," he says.

"He has been unable to retire," longtime friend, fellow pharmacist and Frosty's "golf wife," Rick Sahli says.

"He has his fingers in more pots than you can imagine," Sahli says. "Frosty has to be involved. He needs to feel relevant, like he is still in the game. And he loves doing all the stuff he's doing. He is the most generous person I have ever met. He would give you the shirt off his back and the skin to go with it if you needed it. It is part of his nature."

Also, part of the nature of both Frosty and Vicki: To wear Beaver orange.

"He has a running bet with a lawyer friend, Jeff Hasson, about the Civil War football game each year," friend Dennis Rogers says. "Whoever loses has to wear the other team's colors."

"Never seen bigger Beaver fans," CSG president John Brase says. "I asked Vicki if she wears Beaver gear 365 days a year. She said, 'No, only 364. Not on Christmas.'"

There is gratitude toward his alma mater.

"Oregon State accepted me after not having the best grades at Willamette and allowed me to get into a graduate program in the college of pharmacy," Frosty says. "It gave me a profession that saved my life. I could have been drafted, sent over to Vietnam or some other place and ended up in a body bag. And it introduced me to my wife."

Ah, Frosty and Vicki. Look what they have accomplished! Look what is still ahead.

"We are still growing," Frosty says. After what he has been through, who is to doubt him?

ABOUT THE AUTHOR

KERRY EGGERS is a journalist/author who wrote sports for Portland newspapers for 45 years. He worked for the *Oregon Journal* from 1975-82, at *The Oregonian* from 1982-2000 and at the *Portland Tribune* from 2001- 2020. Eggers is a six-time the National Sports Media Association's Oregon Sportswriter of the Year, winning in 1981, 1997, 2000, 2003, 2011 and 2018.

Through his career, Eggers covered a variety of major events, including two Summer Olympic Games, four Super Bowls, a World Series, two major-league All-Star Games, five College World Series, two national championship football games, three Davis Cup ties, a golf U.S. Open, a Pro Bowl, six track and field Olympic trials and many NBA Finals and NBA All-Star games.

Eggers is past president of Track & Field Writers of America and recipient of the Jesse Abrahamson Award as the nation's top track and field writer. In 2014, he was honored with the "DNA Award" — recognizing "extraordinary passion and dedication to sport in Oregon" — at the Oregon Sports Awards.

This is Eggers' 10th book. The others: *Blazers Profiles* (1991); *Against the World* (1993, with co-author Dwight Jaynes); *Wherever You May Be: The Bill Schonely Story* (1999); *Clyde "The Glide" Drexler: My Life in Basketball* (2004); *Oregon State University Football Vault* (2009); *The Civil War Rivalry: Oregon vs. Oregon State* (2014); *Jail Blazers: How the Portland Trail Blazers Became the Bad Boys of Basketball* (2018), *Jerome Kersey: Overcoming the Odds* (2021) and *Wherever You May Be … Now: The Bill Schonely Story* (2023).

Acknowledgements

Frosty Comer is a well-known figure in Oregon State athletics. He is a generous donor to OSU sports, served for several years as a member of the "Our Beaver Nation" advisory board and was president of the board for a two-year term. In addition, we had a close mutual friend — Bud Ossey, perhaps the most famous Beaver sports fan ever who passed away at the age of 101 in 2021.

It was at an event where Ossey was honored by the Society of American Military Engineers with a 75-year pin as one of the national organization's "distinguished Fellows" a month before his death that I met Comer. We had a good if quick chat, and he expressed interest in buying one of my books. He also said he had a proposition for me and invited me to his home for a visit.

During the visit, he expressed interest in me writing a book about his family, his career and Cook Solutions Group, for which he serves as chairman of the board. We talked about my website, and I asked if he had interest in being a sponsor. He said yes — he would be interested in being its primary sponsor. And maybe we could make a deal. Cook Solutions Group would sponsor the website, and I would write a book for him.

My only reluctance was the subject matter — and I don't mean Frosty Comer, an interesting guy if I've ever met one. His career, however, has been all about pharmacy and the military. Those subjects weren't just out of my wheelhouse, they would be like talking a foreign language.

But we swung a deal, and off he went, sailing through his story with the finesse of a surgeon and the speed of a race-car driver. When I told him it would be beneficial to visit the ghost town of Comertown,

Mont., where his great-grandparents homesteaded in the early 20th century, Frosty didn't bat an eye. We were on a flight to the site within 10 days.

Frosty's memory is remarkable, his love for what he does intense, and his get-er-done philosophy and drive daunting. "Frosty and (wife) Vicki both have a motor," OSU associate athletic director Jeff Pivic says. "There is not a challenge either one of them go away from."

The project was completed despite Frosty, indeed, speaking a foreign language as he delivered military and pharmacy terms and acronyms I'd never heard of. He was patient, though, and good to work with. He is a fun guy, and very popular with friends and colleagues, who had plenty of stories to tell.

Thanks to all of those friends and colleagues of the Comers who took the time to be interviewed and provide insight for the book. Thanks to Frosty and Vicki for their time and good spirits throughout the project. Thanks to their daughters, Molly Angelo and Wendy Lambert, for their contributions. A special thanks to Brian Cook, CEO and brainchild of Cook Solutions Group, for his insights on the Comer family and the genesis of CSG.

Through three decades of writing books, I have not had a publisher as professional and easy to work with as Wayne Dementi. Thanks, Wayne, for your help and guidance in getting this book published in timely fashion. Thanks also to his graphic artist extraordinaire, Jayne Hushen, who is welcome to work on any future book project of mine.

Thank you, too, to my wife, Stephanie Holladay, whose careful copyediting eye caught enough errors to make me wonder how I could miss so many things. Nice work, Sweetie.

INDEX

A

Abbott, Glenn 33
Adams, Bud, 25
Adelphi University 57
Albany, Ore., 11
Ambrose, N.D. 3
Angelo, Aaron 163
Angelo, Brady 163
Angelo, Joey 163, 170
Angelo, Molly Comer, 11, 42, 87-88, 108, 155, 158, 162-163, 165-172, 184
Angelo, Tony 163
Ann Arbor, Mich. 130-131
Arlotta, John 149-150
Apria 151-153
Aurora, Colo., 140, 144

B

Baltimore, Md., 118-119
Bandon, Ore., 54
Barnes, Scott 203
Beaverton, Ore., 64, 87, 155, 157
Beaverton High School 87, 157, 160-161, 175, 183, 186, 190
Bend, Ore. 112
Bennett, David 144
Berlin, Germany 91
Bert, Jeff 93-94, 99-101
Bird Island, Minn., 57
Bishop, Tyler 199
Bismarck, N.D., 10
Briley, Brian 150
Boerne, Tex., 145

Boise, Ida., 112, 176
Bowen, Tom, 27
Brady, Al, 67-68
Brase, John 175, 190-191, 211
Buell, Joan, 70-71
Buell, Tom, 70
Bykonen, Judy, 6-7

C

California, University of Berkeley 131
California, University of Davis 133
Cash, Kay 119
Castles, Jim, 73, 82
Castles, John, 73, 82-85
Catlin Gabel School 70
Centralia, Wash. 112
Cent-Wise Drugs 11, 36-37, 56
Chelan, Wash., 66
Cheney, Dick 97
Chicago, Ill. 123
Cincinnati, Ohio 176
Clackamas High School 200
Clark, Cabot 49-51, 91
Clark, Paige 205-208
Coberly, Ron, 53
Collell, Karen 117, 121-122
Columbia, S.C. 145
Columbus, Ohio 145
Comer, Carl, 2,
Comer, Clayton, 2, 9-12, 27
Comer, Connie, 17, 20, 23,
Comer, Connie Graves (Frosty's mother), 12-13, 17, 20, 71
Comer, Mayme, 10-12

Comer, Percival, 2,
Comer, Phi, 1-4, 9
Comer, Vicki, 29, 32-37, 39-42, 46, 54, 56, 79, 81-82, 87, 92, 147, 156, 158-161, 167-168, 183, 193-197, 199, 207-208
Comer, Walker, 2
Comer, William Blair "Bill," 10, 12-16, 18, 21-23, 27,
Comer, William Walter, 1-2, 4, 9
Comertown, 3-5, 7, 20
Comertown Coyotes, 4
Comer Park 4
Cook, Brian 11, 156-163, 165-181, 184-188, 190-191
Cook, Craig 156, 159, 175, 184-185
Cook, Donna 156
Cook, Kristie 156
Cook, Monte 156
Cook, Ralph 185
Cook, Shauna 169
Cook Community Builders 180-181
Cook Security Group 166, 169-171, 175
Cook Solutions Group 172-180, 183-191, 211
Coon Chicken Inn, 14
Coos Bay, Ore., 53-54, 94
Coquille, Ore., 54
Coram Health Care 114-115, 118, 120-123, 133, 136, 139, 141-146, 149-153, 168, 202
Cornell University 131, 133
Corvallis, Ore., 36-37, 45, 47, 189, 210,
Cottage Grove, Ore., 37
Craig, Rich 161

Creighton University 57
Crowley, Dan, 139, 142, 149
Crumpacker, Nancy 132
Crystal City, Va. 119, 121
Culbertson, Mont., 3, 5

D

Danielski, Linn, 46-47, 143, 146
Day, Douglas, 23-24
De Carolis, Bob 202
Denny, Marjorie, 11
Deloitte and Touche 163, 169, 171
Des Moines, Wash., 11
Dick, Ken 90
Dorge, Robert, 28
Drake, Dick, 54
Durham, N.C. 115
Duvall, Robert 120

E

Edes, Tom 122
Egging, Paulette, 59, 81-82, 84-86
English, Woody 107
Escobar, Aaron 203
Eugene, Ore., 50, 106, 109, 210

F

Far West Federal Bank 79, 81, 161
Fischer, Fred 210
Florence, Ore., 54
Forks, Wash., 11
Forsythe, Charlie 167
Fort Knox, Ky., 30
Fort Lewis, Wash., 12-13, 35, 46, 90, 105, 126

Fort Ord, Calif., 50
Fort Sill, Okla., 146
Fort Vancouver, Wash., 51, 91, 96
Frankfurt, Germany 90
Fred Meyer Foundation 71-72
Frenzel, Bill, 32, 36
Frenzel, Brylanne, 36
Fresno, Calif., 11

G

Glynn, Jim 115
Gold Beach, Ore., 54
Gonzalez, Roberto 146, 148-149
Good Samaritan Hospital, 56-58, 62-63, 65-66, 70-71, 74-75, 77-81, 85-86, 95, 117, 210
Graves, Eunice, 15
Graves, Vern, 15
Graybeal, Richard, 53
Greenleaf, Abbott 151
Greenleaf, Dan 151-152
Gregory, Christine 150
Gulf War 85

H

Hanby, Wayne, 10
Hartnett, Mike 86
Harvard University 131, 133
Hasson, Jeff 211
Haubner, Ruth 145, 149
Healthinfusion 113
Heidelberg, Germany 96
Hellegaard, Marvel, 6-7
Hemlock Society 130
Henningsen Family Foundation 71

Hines, Ill. 123
Hopewell House 71-74, 82-83, 110

J

Jenkins, Joey 201
Jenkins, Ron 122
Johnson, Doreen, 6
Johnson, Jay, 64, 81
Johnson, Linda, 64, 81
Johnson, Richard, 6-7

K

KBCH radio 18-21
KEX radio 19, 21-22
KPOJ radio 27
Kelly, Mike 146
Kennedy Grade School, 17
Kinsman, John 82
Klamath Falls, Ore. 106-107, 109, 112
Knight, Phil 171, 172

L

La Grande, Ore. 107
Lambert, Blake 183
Lambert, Wendy Comer, 42, 87-88, 155-156, 158, 160, 163, 183-184
Lambert, Zachary 183
Las Vegas, Nev., 141
Lebanon, Ore. 11, 36-37
Lebanon High School, 39
Lee, Barbara Combs 130
Legacy Health Care, 74, 79
Lehman, Milt 81-82, 85
Leininger, Connie, 33, 54
Leininger, Curly, 32-33, 53

Leininger, Terry, 33
Lemon, Chet 33
Lincoln City, Ore., 18, 209
Livorno, Italy 41
Loomis, Bob 107-108
Loveless, Mark 109-111
Lucas, Maurice 187
Lutz Snyder Realty 87

M

Madison High School, 21
Marshfield High School, 54
Mayes, Tommy 145-146
McCall, Tom 35
McCarthy, James 100-101
McCormack, David 133
Mead, Mary Jo 119, 122-123
Meadows, Greg 152
Medford, Ore., 106-107, 109, 112, 210
Mendez, Henry, 44
Meyer, Debbie 139, 141-142, 149, 153
Miami, Fla. 113
Michigan, University of 131
Mitchel, Jon, 53
Milbrett, Tiffany 88
Miller, Jack, 70
Milne, Casey Comer 14-15, 66, 81, 132
Mitchell, Amy 119
Moda Center 177
Monmouth, Ore., 36
Montec Security 162, 171
Monterey, Calif., 50
Mosler Security 160-161, 171
Mount Hood Ski Patrol, 64, 82
Murdock Foundation 73

Murdock, Jack, 73

N

Naehr, Larry 141
Nashville, Tenn. 120
New Orleans, La., 120
Nettles, Heyward Harry, 44
Neu, Carter 181-182
Neu, Lucas 187
Neu, Marilyn 181-182
Neu, Ramsay 187
Neu, Randy 175, 181-182, 186-188, 190
Neu, Tracy 187
Nichols, Bob, 66
Nichols, Kim Comer, 17, 66-69, 71, 130, 132
Norfolk, Va., 12
North Bend, Ore., 53-54
North Bend High School, 33

O

Oden, Greg 187
Ohio State University 131
Oliva, Steve 106
Olson, Beverley, 6-7
Operation Desert Shield/Storm 89, 93, 99
Option Care 106, 109
Oregon Board of Pharmacy 90
Oregon College of Education, 36
Oregon Health Sciences University 107, 113
Oregon State University, 27-29, 31, 33-34, 45, 47, 49, 51, 53-54, 60, 81, 87, 92,

108, 158, 162-163, 183, 189, 199-206, 208-210, 212
Oregon, University of 92, 108, 186, 190

P

Pallor, Bob, 74
Patrick, Vern, 11
Patterson, Jim 203
Payne, Richard, 24
Pendleton, Ore. 107
Peters, Tom 80, 202
Peterson, Chris, 6,
Philomath, Ore., 36
Pigeon, Bill, 28-29
Civic, Jeff 203-205
Plentywood, Mont., 3, 5
Pocatello, Ida., 11
Ponderosa Enterprise, 79
Portland, Ore., 11, 14, 17, 30, 48, 57, 67, 71-72, 81, 105, 112, 115, 141, 157
Portland Community College 160-161
Portland State University 70
Portland Thorns 177
Portland Timbers 177
Portland Trail Blazers 177, 186-187
Princeton University 133
Provencher, Ken 107-108
Providence Park 177
Purdue University 57

Q

Quantico, Va., 12
Quaranta, Mike 81

R

Ramsey, Barb 146-149
Ramsey, Jim 146-149
Rash, Jim 81
Reagan, Ronald 35
Redmond, Ore., 11
Reedsport, Ore., 54
Reno, Nev., 176
Richmond, Va. 119
Rogers, Dennis, 49-50, 91-92, 211
Rogers, Lou Anne, 50
Roggi, Mike 96
Rome, Italy, 41
Rose City Grade School, 15
Roseburg, Ore., 21
Ross, Larry, 197

S

Sahli, Rick, 59-62, 211
St. John, Terri 145, 149
St. Louis, Mo. 120, 145, 150
St. Vincent Hospital 210-211
Salazar, Teresa 189-190
Sacramento, Calif. 150, 176
Salem, Ore., 50
Salt Lake City, Utah 145, 150
San Antonio, Texas, 39-40, 143, 145, 148
San Diego, Calif. 120
Sanger, Jim, 57-59, 63, 80, 86
Schnabel, Gary 90, 106
Schoeps, Dan 122
Schultz, Noah 202
Schwarzkopf, Norman 99
Searle, Larry 126

Seattle, Wash. 112, 126, 141, 176
Seiter, Jerry 142, 146
Sheridan County Museum, 6
Simpson, Robert 146, 148
Sisson, Harriet, 28, 47
Slingball 181
Slotfeldt, Marilyn 85-86
Smith, Rick 136
Sobel, Steve 150
South Salem High School
Southern California, University of 35
Southwest Oregon Community College, 33
Spoelstra, Erik 186
Spokane, Wash. 112
Springfield, Ore., 11
Stansbury, Todd 203
Stark, Pete 106, 114
Stuttgart, Germany 90, 93-94, 96, 98, 100, 102, 105
Sumption, Jeannine 81
Sunset High School 82

T

Tacoma, Wash., 10, 12-13, 112, 141
Taft High School, 19-20, 209
Tampa Bay, Fla., 125
Tange, Pat, 6, 8
Taylor, Misty 136
Tektronix, 73
Tillery, Steve 81
Torgerson, Otto, 6-8
Trento, Italy, 41
Trunkey, Donald 99
Tualatin, Ore., 114, 132, 200

U

Urban, Jane 81
Utter, Jess, 19
Utter, Nettie, 19

V

Van Buren, Linda, 66, 68
Vancouver, Wash., 47, 49-51, 89, 106, 126
Vicenza, Italy, 40-41, 43, 45, 87, 91, 93, 155, 209
Vistler, Joe, 6
Vital Choice 80-81, 83-85, 88-89, 105-107, 109, 111, 113-114
Vogel, Donna 119, 124

W

Ward, Tom 117
Washington, Claudell 33
Washington, University of 82, 131, 133
Washington D.C. 120, 123
W.R. Vezina, 3
Webster, Bob 21,
Wetzel, John 187
Whitetail, Mont., 3
Willamette University, 12, 23-25, 27-28, 30, 35
Willis, Sandy 146
Williston, N.D., 1, 5
Wilson, Preston, 84
Wilson High School, 21, 23
Wise, Rick 21
Woodburn, Ore., 27

Y

Yunker, Frank 124-125

Z

Zacher, Brian 200-201
Zepeda, Gloria 199-200

FROSTY'S NO SNOWMAN

Oregon State University College of Pharmacy

All profits and donations from the sale of this book will go to the
Oregon State University Foundation for the
COMER FAMILY SCHOLARSHIP
in the support of pharmacy students who are in or have been
in the military.

https://give.fororegonstate.org/PL1Uv3Fkug

1) visit fororegonstate.org
2) Click Give Online Now
3) Type Comer in the I want to Give to field.
4) Click on Comer Family Scholarship and make your donation